Pocketguide to

PENNSYLVANIA HATCHES

Charles Meck and Paul Weamer

HEADWATER BOOKS

STACKPOLE BOOKS

Published by
HEADWATER BOOKS
531 Harding Street
New Cumberland, PA 17070
www.headwaterbooks.com

STACKPOLE BOOKS
5067 Ritter Road
Mechanicsburg, PA 17055
www.stackpolebooks.com

Printed in the United States of America

First edition

Distributed by NATIONAL BOOK NETWORK

Cover design by Tracy Patterson
Cover photographs by Jay Nichols
All fly pattern photos by Jay Nichols
Insect photos by Paul Weamer unless otherwise indicated

Library of Congress Control Number: 2008938124

ISBN: 978-0-9793460-5-7

Contents

Acknowledgments

More than thirty years ago I gave a talk on the hatches in Baltimore, Maryland, to about forty people. Ernest Schwiebert sat in the front row and listened intensely. I was probably more nervous at the talk than any other I have ever presented. Why? In my formative years of fly fishing—in the 1950s and 1960s—his book *Matching the Hatch* was my bible. I read and reread the book almost daily. It was because of him and his seminal book that I became deeply interested in the hatches. Thanks also to R. Wills Flowers of Florida A & M University in Tallahassee, Florida. Since 1976 Wills has identified difficult mayfly species for me, including most of those in *Meeting and Fishing the Hatches*.

Charlie Meck

Thank you to John Miller, a terrific insect photographer, for providing us with several mayfly and caddisfly photographs, and to Headwater Books for giving me the honor of cowriting this book with one of my mentors and friends, Charlie Meck. Thank you to Jay Nichols for your friendship and for shooting all of the fly pattern photographs for this book. Your hard work and dedication makes each of the projects you begin better by the time it is finished.

Thanks most of all to my wife, Ruthann—for all of the times you wanted to work on our new house, to take walks along the creek, or just to spend time together when I could not because I was locked away writing or shooting photographs. Once again, your sacrifices have made my efforts possible.

Paul Weamer

Pennsylvania is blessed with hundreds of miles of prime trout water. Paul Weamer gets ready to release a nice Fishing Creek brown caught on top.

JAY NICHOLS PHOTO

1 Using This Guide

Pennsylvania has more miles of rivers and streams than any other state except Alaska. Much of this water is prime trout habitat, with clean, cold water and amazing insect populations to keep fish fat and healthy. This book is about the most important insects that Pennsylvania trout eat and the fly patterns that imitate them.

Many great books have been written about Eastern hatches, and we do not intend to replace them. But this book was written solely for Pennsylvania anglers. We provide detailed information about where, when, and how the insects hatch as well as tactics and tips for imitating them with flies. We also provide phenological information to show the relationship between aquatic hatches and the plants that grow along the stream.

The hatch charts include all the major trout stream insects in the state. Though we also include some minor ones (indicated with asterisks), we have not included in-depth discussions or photographs for them. It would be impossible to include all of the bugs trout eat and still keep the book small enough so that it can be easily carried streamside. To that end, we had to omit some locally important insects that do not have a broad enough range through the state.

We provide thorough descriptions of the life cycles for these major insects but in most instances only include photographs of the subadult (dun) or adult (spinner) stages. We've done this for two reasons. First, it's easier for most anglers to identify a hatch by looking at the bugs that are tucked in streamside vegetation, floating on the water, or flying. Turning over rocks to see which nymphs

JAY NICHOLS PHOTO

On pressured streams such as Clark Creek, near Harrisburg, fish often demand precise imitations and perfect presentations.

are living there is a poor way to find and collect nymphs. As soon as you lift a rock, water swirls around it, removing any bug that wasn't able to hold tightly. To properly collect and identify larvae or nymphs, you need seine nets and magnification devices, baggage most people don't want to carry with them onstream.

Second, it's easier for the untrained eye to see physical similarities and differences of adult or subadult insects than those of larvae or nymphs. Most anglers can differentiate between stonefly nymphs, mayfly nymphs, and caddis larvae. But it's much more complicated to distinguish the exact species, unless you're looking at a winged adult or subadult. Mayflies don't reach full, sexually mature adulthood until they become spinners. But because mayfly spinners of varying species can also look similar, most of our photos highlight the mayfly subimago, or dun, stage.

ABOUT THE ENTRIES

1. The most common name of the insect in Pennsylvania.
2. Other common names for the bug.
3. Genus and species, followed by previous (prev.) names.
4. Approximate emergence dates and times of day.
5. Approximate hook size range. Assume standard shank hooks unless otherwise noted. Approximate millimeter range is included because of the variance among hook models. Keep in mind that the size of bugs can vary from stream to stream, and even on the same stream, size can vary widely.

Description. Colors, number of tails, and other major identifying features, including any differences between male and female. This information provides the basics for both identification and replication at the tying bench. Includes notes on any other insects that this one resembles.

Emergence. A description of when the insect hatches, including flowers and trees that are blooming and other hatches that might appear at the same time. These dates are just estimates and are subject to variables in the weather, water temperature, and type of stream, among other things. See chapter 3, Timing the Hatches, for a discussion of some of these variables. Time of day is also an average or description of "typical." When it is cloudy and cool, Hendricksons can hatch all day on some streams; on a bright sunny day, the hatch may only last a short period.

Behavior and Tactics. Any behavior that is important to anglers and tactics for imitating that behavior. We often suggest flies and how to fish them, but you should refer to the section "Fly Patterns and Color," page 6, and match your fly selection based on the conditions and your observations of the naturals.

Notes. Additional information of interest to anglers.

Premier Hatches. The rivers with the best hatches of the insect. Some rivers, like the Upper Delaware and Penns Creek, have premier status for many of the hatches, but we tried to spread them around the state. On many waters across the state, rivers and streams lose hatches and gain new ones, especially those recovering

JAY NICHOLS PHOTO

Grannom hatches provide the first blizzard hatches of spring.

from pollution. Some bugs are more intolerant than others to pollution and are indicators of water quality. Quill Gordon's requires high-quality water and disappear at any sign of pollution. Conversely, Sulphurs are one of the first mayfly species to appear in a cleaned-up stream. The state's streams are changing constantly—some degrading, others improving—and hatches change with them, so the Premier Hatches entries are not carved in stone.

FLY PATTERNS AND COLOR

For each entry we provide only one fly pattern, but that does not mean that pattern is always the best choice. We selected that pattern because it is one of the most effective for the hatch, but all of the patterns in this book represent styles of tying that can and should be adapted to match the wide variety of species we list in this book. We include both hackled patterns (traditional Catskill-style patterns, thorax-style flies, caddis and stoneflies with palmered-hackle bodies) and flush-floating ones (flies with no hackle or clipped hackle on the bottom so that they ride right on the surface of the water). Often in the text we refer to general pattern styles such as flush-floating or hackled, or Truform style or parachute style.

Selecting the right fly pattern takes time to master, but here are a few important considerations.

Location. Where in the water column are the naturals floating; where are the fish feeding? If the fish are feeding just under the surface, and showing the bulging rises characteristic of that, than you are better off fishing a low-riding fly or emerger rather than a heavily hackled pattern that rides high on the water.

Pressure. For unpressured fish and mountain streams, you can get away with a few different flies representing the general shapes of mayflies and caddis. A good fastwater fly should float well and be durable and easy to see.

Water Type. In fast water and riffles, a hackle pattern

JAY NICHOLS PHOTO

Spring creeks and slow water require different patterns than tumbling freestone streams. For slow water and finicky fish, choose a sparse fly; for fast water, choose files that float well.

When fishing for brook trout, any high-floating fly such as a Wulff or Stimulator works well.

JAY NICHOLS PHOTO

floats higher, keeping the fly floating longer and making it easier for an angler to see, and the fish are often less selective. In slow water, where trout have more time to scrutinize a fly, flush-floating patterns are usually a better choice.

Time of Day. In the bright light of midday or afternoon, you may need to use a sparser, more accurate pattern than if you are fishing a hatch or spinnerfall in low light. On bright days, especially when the water is clear, you might also have to fish longer leaders and more delicate tippets. Fish as short a leader and as strong a tippet as you can get away with.

Weather. If it is windy and duns are being blown across the surface of the water, a hackled pattern that can skitter on the surface may outperform a flush-floating one. If it is cold, duns generally take longer to dry their wings, and a flush-floating pattern works well. When the weather is warm, duns move more, which can be better imitated with a hackled pattern. In bad light, a high-riding pattern or one tied with a highly visible parachute post is a distinct advantage over a drab pattern that rides low in the surface. In the silver sheen of glare on the water, a fly with a black wingpost is easier to see than one with a white post.

Fish-Eye View. When choosing a pattern, consider what the fish sees. When trout are feeding on mayfly duns, they do not care about the color of the back of the bug. They only see the belly, and that is what you want to match. It's also important to consider the size of the bug and its wing profile.

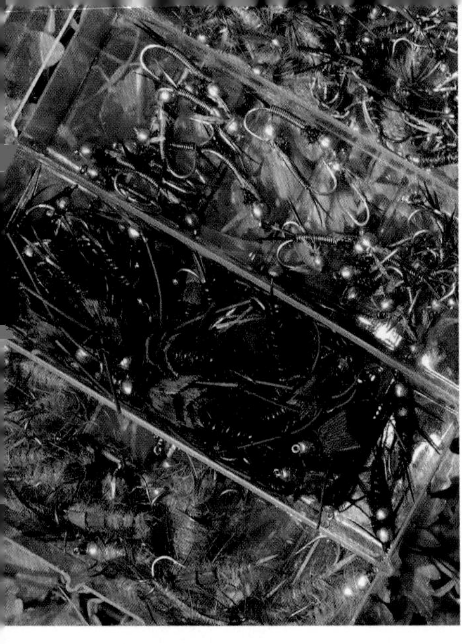

JAY NICHOLS PHOTO

Nymphs are vital for consistent success, but you can get by with a limited selection. Carry many of them, however, because you lose a lot of them when you are fishing them correctly—on the bottom.

Note about Nymphs

By not including photos of nymphs or patterns with the level of variety as dry flies, we do not intend to underestimate the importance of becoming a good nymph fisherman to consistently catch Pennsylvania's trout. We fish nymphs often, and they are critical for success in the winter and early spring before the fish start looking toward the surface. But we believe that the basic nymph pattern selection that we've included can effectively cover most hatch-matching nymphing situations. The nymph fisherman is usually imitating just one stage of the aquatic insect's life, whereas dry flies can encompass several stages—emerger, dun, egg layer, and spent spinner—as well as the adult terrestrial. In most situations, fish also seem to feed less selectively on underwater food items. We include descriptions of each species of caddis larvae and mayfly and stonefly nymphs so that anglers can adapt our basic nymph selection to match many of these insects.

Color

Professional entomologists (the only real bug experts) place no emphasis on a fly's color when determining its species because insect color is too variable, even among the same species, to provide positive identification. Water chemistry, diet of the nymphs, and minute genetic differences (are your father, mother, or one of your sibling's skin tones slightly different than your own?) can create variances, dramatic or subtle, in insect coloration, making it impossible for anglers to imitate each mayfly's exact color.

Slate Drakes are a good example of color variation. Some Slate Drakes are gray with a hint of olive or maroon on their undersides. Other Slate Drakes are reddish mahogany in color, while yet others are bright green or olive when they first emerge. In addition to the factors mentioned above that can change a bug's color, most mayflies experience slight color changes after emerging, slowly darkening as they are exposed to the air. So mayflies that are hatching right in front of you may be lighter, or paler, than those that have hatched upstream and floated down to you.

Because of all these variances in color, the colors in the insect descriptions and fly pattern recipes are just guidelines. If you select the right pattern that matches the size of the insect, and make a good presentation, matching the overall shade of the bug is generally the best you can do. Here's a tip: generally speaking, mayflies that emerge in the spring and fall are dark shades, and bugs that emerge in the summer are light shades.

JAY NICHOLS PHOTO

When fishing in fast pocketwater, it is often effective to fish a small nymph tied to the bend of your dry fly.

Pennsylvania has a wide range of water types, making for diverse trout fishing opportunities. One day you can fish a mountain freestone stream for brookies or try your luck with finicky spring creek trout. These diverse fisheries offer year-round opportunities to catch fish.

JAY NICHOLS PHOTO

2 Pennsylvania's Trout Waters

The variety of trout water—freestones, limestones, tailwaters (or combinations of these)—in the state creates a lot of diversity in the types, length, and timing of the hatches. It is important to have a basic understanding of these different types of waters.

Freestone streams are the most common in Pennsylvania, and they are especially predominant in the northern half of the state. They often begin in mountains and flow through sandstone or shale. Unlike many limestone streams, most freestone streams lack large springs at their headwaters. Freestone streams face several challenges as viable trout streams. They often cope with acidic or near-neutral waters with a pH of seven or lower. The pH is a measure of alkalinity or acidity. A reading of seven is considered neutral. Any reading over seven is alkaline, and lower than seven is acidic. Freestone streams often have high seasonal flows during early spring and low flows throughout much of the summer.

Freestone streams also suffer from temperature extremes, flowing under a mantel of ice in the winter and suffering from high water temperatures in the summer, which can make or break fishing at this time of the year. Tricos and Yellow Drakes hatch in many freestoners in July, and if the waters are cool enough, the hatches provide excellent midsummer match-the-hatch opportunities. However, temperatures in freestoners like Pine Creek in Lycoming County and Kettle Creek in Potter County often rise into the high seventies and low eighties in July and August. Trout exit most of these warmer waters and search out springs or cooler tributaries.

Although freestone streams have fluctuating flows and temperatures, they provide a huge diversity of aquatic insects. Hatches common on freestones include most of the early hatches like the Blue Quill, Hendrickson, and Quill Gordon and late May hatches like the Green Drake and Slate Drake.

Limestone streams originate in valleys and flow over limestone or dolomite bedrock. As they flow underground, these waters dissolve calcium carbonate, which makes them highly alkaline. They often begin above ground with a heavy slug of water from a large spring like the one at the source of Spruce Creek and Penns Creek in central Pennsylvania and on Falling Springs Branch near Chambersburg. The pH on these waters often ranges between 7.5 and 8.5. Because this pH is higher (alkaline), these streams offer more food for the residing trout population than freestone streams.

Temperatures at the source frequently are 54 degrees in Pennsylvania. To determine fairly accurately the temperature of a large limestone spring at its source, simply find the average mean temperature of the area. Through the seasons, when freestoners are suffering through the extremes of cold or heat, these springs stabilize fluctuations in water and temperatures. In summer, water temperatures often remain in the sixties with a fairly good flow throughout the season. In winter, many limestone spring creeks remain open because of the moderate water temperatures. Limestone streams often have profuse hatches with the three top being *Baetis,* Sulphurs, and Tricos. Limestone waters, because they begin in fertile valleys, can frequently flow through rich, intensely cultivated farmlands, which can produce heavy sedimentation.

Scuds and sowbugs (which are crustaceans) are important spring creek trout foods (though they are also found in tailwaters and freestone streams). They spend their entire life underwater, living beneath rocks or in aquatic vegetation. Scuds, also called freshwater shrimp, have olive, tan, gray, orange, or amber bodies and legs. Capture specimens to find the most prevalent color. Scuds turn an orangeish color when they die, and many anglers catch trout with orange scud patterns, which may also be taken for egg patterns. Scuds are good swimmers and prefer cold, alkaline waters.

JAY NICHOLS PHOTO

Big Spring near Newville is one of many limestone spring creeks in the state that offer year-round opportunities to catch fish on dry flies.

Above: *Sowbug, or pillbug.*
Right: *Scud, or freshwater shrimp.*

To imitate them dead-drift #12–18 scud patterns through riffles or near pockets of aquatic vegetation or strip them with quick, short strokes to imitate swimming scuds.

Sowbugs, also called pillbugs, are gray. Unlike scuds, which are good swimmers, sowbugs generally crawl along aquatic vegetation—their preferred habitat. To imitate them, dead-drift a #12–20 Day's Burnt Back Sowbug and Walt's Worm through riffles and near pockets of aquatic vegetation. Sowbugs are generally less prolific than scuds, but trout feed on them where they are found.

Beadhead Olive Scud and Day's Burnt Back Sowbug.
See recipes in Appendix, page 147–48.

Tailwaters have been almost totally neglected in the state. However, with increasingly warmer summer temperatures, this type of trout water will become more important. Tailwaters are dammed streams (either freestone or limestone in nature, though most in Pennsylvania are freestone) with outflows that come from the bottom of impounded lakes. In many ways, they are similar to limestone streams, flowing cool through the summer with a steady flow.

The depth of the lake is critical to the productivity of the tailwater and to provide cool water, a bottom release should be at least 75 feet deep. Tulpehocken Creek, a Berks County limestone stream, flows into Blue Marsh Dam and then flows out of a bottom release. However, the gate is only 45 feet deep so it doesn't enjoy the cooler temperature it could if the lake were deeper. Temperatures in this quasi-tailwater often rise into the high seventies during the

summer. The bottom release on the East Branch Clarion River in northwestern Pennsylvania is a totally different story. It flows from a 175-foot-deep gate. Temperatures on this freestone remain in the low sixties throughout the hot summer months. Tailwaters can be the salvation of trout fishing in the state because the releases keep the downstream water cool throughout the summer and warmer during the winter. A bottom release on a normally warmwater stream like the Allegheny River at Kinzua can transform a warm smallmouth bass river into a truly great trout fishery.

But the artificial water temperatures created by tailwaters can hugely impact aquatic hatches. If little water is being released in the spring, the river section closest to the dam may be low and warm up quicker than downriver sections. Aquatic hatches during these conditions may actually begin upstream, before the same hatch occurs downriver. This hatch progression is the opposite of what usually occurs in freestone and limestone streams. Water nearest the dams is often very cold, limiting insect diversity to a few species that can tolerate the cold water, like Blue-Winged Olives and Sulphurs. Downstream, as the water warms, the more diverse aquatic insect species will populate it.

Paul Weamer fishes a nice pool on the Little Juniata River.

Charlie Meck with a nice brown that fell for a Trico spinner.

JAY NICHOLS PHOTO

3 Timing the Hatches

Hatches and spinnerfalls are influenced by water temperature and air temperature; therefore, we can only provide average emergence times and dates based on our years of observations. In addition to average temperatures for different locations in the state, abnormally warm or cool weather patterns, water levels, or even daily weather (whether it is sunny or cloudy) affects the timing and duration of the hatches. This is where understanding how flower and tree blooms correspond to the timing of hatches becomes important because those plants are influenced by the weather in a similar way as aquatic insects. The hatches themselves also provide a clue about what is to come. You can guess when a particular hatch will occur based on other bugs that have emerged.

Hatch dates and times vary tremendously in the three types of waters covered in the previous chapter. Waters in limestone streams and tailwaters are moderate in the winter and cold in the summer, variations that can dramatically affect the timing and duration of the hatches. Hatches on tailwaters often appear a bit later or longer in the season or at a different time of the day than on freestone streams. For example, the Pale Evening Dun (*Ephemerella dorothea*) may appear every day for over two months in the afternoon on the West Branch of the Delaware River. *Baetis* can hatch every month of the year on a spring creek like Big Spring, in Newville.

Hatch dates also vary according to geographical location in the state. Hendricksons often start hatching on Bald Eagle Creek in central Pennsylvania around April 15. On Oswayo Creek just north of Coudersport, that same hatch normally begins around April 20.

Above: *Forsythia along Penns Creek, blooming during the Grannom hatch. This photo was taken May 3, during a year in which hatches and blooms were about two weeks later than usual.* Left: *Dame's rocket that has been in bloom for awhile. Note that it has four petals, whereas phlox has five.*

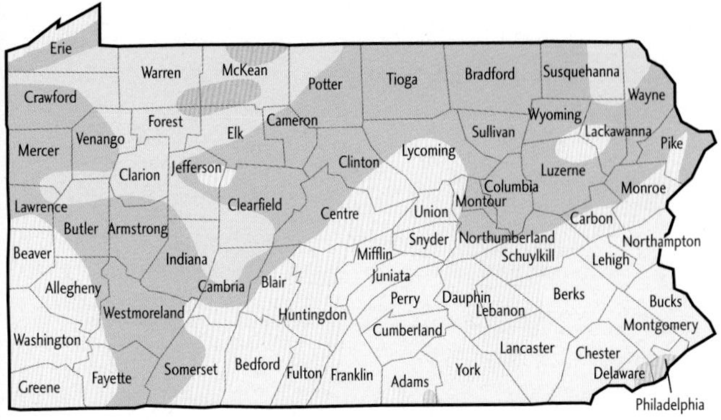

This map, adapted from the USDA hardiness zone map, shows an estimated variation in the hatch dates we provide in this book based on geographic location. White: Average; Yellow: Subtract five days; Dark Green: Add five days; Light Green: Add ten days; Purple: Add fifteen days; Light Purple: subtract ten days.

Why the difference? Hatches vary from north to south because of the weather. It's a bit colder in Coudersport than it is in the Bald Eagle Valley, and hatches reflect that difference. The emergence map, which is an adaptation of the hardiness zone map for planting compiled by the United States Department of Agriculture, is designed to compensate for this disparity. If temperatures vary from region to region, then so does the timing of the hatches.

On this map, based on average temperatures for each of these zones, the colors indicate whether the hatch dates we provide are averages or if you need to adjust them by adding or subtracting days. For instance, rivers in the yellow zone, because they are south of the white zone, hatches begin about five days earlier; on rivers in the purple zone, hatches begin about two weeks later.

Changing Hatches

CHARLIE MECK

I first became interested in the hatches in the late 1950s. One of the first hatches I ever encountered was also one of the most spectacular. I traveled along Spring Creek in Centre County one evening in late May 1958 and saw thousands of Coffin Fly spinners in the air along the road. Little did I realize that this was the last time this particular hatch ever appeared on the stream.

I began charting each hatch I've encountered since 1967—more than forty years ago. I kept records of every hatch—when it appeared, what flowers appeared at the same time, water temperatures, and more. In those early years—in the '60s and '70s—I commonly encountered hatches of Hendricksons near the end of April. More recently those same hatches now appear almost a week earlier than they did forty and fifty years ago. In the 1950s, Quill Gordons appeared around April 21 in central Pennsylvania. Now they are more likely to appear almost a week earlier. Why has this occurred?

Winters are warmer now than they were four and five decades ago, which seems to affect the earlier hatches—those appearing in March and April—more than those appearing later. This presents a dilemma for the state's fishing authorities: some of the season's best hatches now appear before Opening Day. They have attempted to cope with this by opening the season in the southeast part of the state one week earlier than the rest of the state.

Global warming has taken its toll on many of the state's marginal streams, many of which have fantastic hatches. The state stocks them a week or two before the season opens—around the end of March or in early April. Fly fishers have about five or six weeks that they can fish many of these waters before they become too warm for trout. Big Pine, Bald Eagle, Loyalsock, and Lycoming

Global warming has taken its toll on many of the state's marginal streams, many of which have fantastic hatches. JACK HANRAHAN PHOTO

creeks, and dozens more throughout the state hold fantastic early season hatches and plenty of planted trout. But they can all become marginal as early as June 1. With global warming, will these streams become void of trout even earlier in the season? What happens to the trout in these waters? If they can find cooler tributaries they may go up them. If they don't, they will probably die. If trout were stocked in these marginal streams in mid-September (after the water cooled a bit), then anglers could fish for them for ten months (September to June) rather than the six weeks (April to June) that they now can. Trout caught before Opening Day would have to be released; anglers could keep trout after Opening Day. This system would benefit all anglers. ■

Green Drake from Penns Creek, near Coburn.

JAY NICHOLS PHOTO

4 Mayflies

Scientists group mayflies in the Order Ephemeroptera, a word that comes from "ephemeral" or "short-lived," because most mayflies live only a few days out of water. Normally mayflies spend approximately 362 days underwater as eggs and nymphs and barely three days or less as duns and spinners. When the female spinner lays the fertilized eggs, it takes several weeks for the larvae (called nymphs) to hatch. Eggs of some species like Tricos and White Flies that are laid in the fall often delay emerging from an egg to a nymph until spring, so the young does not have to endure a long cold winter. Once hatched, nymphs search out and live in specific areas of a stream. Species like the Quill Gordon and March Brown live under rocks; others, like Slate Drakes, live in open view on the bottom of the stream. Many members of the family Ephemerellidae live in aquatic weeds; and Green, Yellow, and Brown Drakes and the White Fly burrow into the substrate or bottom of the stream. Most nymphs feed and grow for about a year before they change into air-breathing duns. Nymphs grow by splitting and shedding their hardened pellicle or nymphal skin in a series of stages called instars.

Most mayflies live underwater for about a year. Some spend a shorter amount of time under the water. Tricos for example, have two generations each year. The eggs of this and similar species laid in late October don't hatch into larvae until May. Once the eggs are fertilized and the nymphs emerge, they live underwater for about seven weeks (forty-eight days). Slate Drake nymphs that emerge in May and June have lived underwater for seven months, while those duns that appear on the surface in September and October live as nymphs only three or four months.

Some mayfly nymphs live underwater for more than a year. Green Drake nymphs, for example, live underwater for two years, so the progeny of Green Drakes emerging in 2009 will emerge in 2011. Many of the larger stoneflies also take two, and some even three, years to appear as adults. This is why you'll sometimes see some especially heavy hatches one year and much less substantial ones the next.

When they are ready to transform from nymphs to air-breathing duns, some change near the bottom, a few midlevel, others at or near the surface, and some crawl onto rocks. Where they change can be critical to the angler. If the nymph changes near the bottom like the Quill Gordon (*Epeorus pleuralis*) and the Pink Lady (*Epeorus vitreus*), then fishing wet flies to imitate the dun rising to the surface can be a dynamite way to catch trout. Other nymphs like the Slate Drake (*Isonychia bicolor*) swim to a rock or to shore and crawl out of the water to emerge. So moving the nymph toward the shore often works when you fish these hatches. The emerging nymph, or the emerger as anglers call it, is one of the two most vulnerable stages of the mayfly life cycle. The other is the spent spinner. Once the emerger sheds its pellicle and becomes an air-breathing subadult, it is called a dun or, as scientists call it, a subimago. The subimago is usually not capable of mating.

When mayfly duns emerge, they rest for a bit on the surface before drying their wings and taking flight. When the water is colder, they ride on the surface longer. If duns are greeted with cool weather and a bit of a drizzle, it's even better for the fly fisher, since both conditions slow down the mayfly considerably. On these inclement, cool, drizzly days, mayflies ride the surface for an extended period and trout feed readily on the surface.

Once the dun takes flight, it heads toward a tree or bush to rest. The mayfly dun rests on a leaf or branch for at least an hour to two and sometimes from up to three days depending, on the species and the weather. On cool spring days, for example, it might take a couple days until the dun changes to a spinner. Some species like the

Mayfly spinner patterns

Poly Wing Spinner, Weamer's Truform Spinner, Stroup's CDC Wing Spinner, Hackle Wing Spinner, and Sunken Spinner. For recipes, see Appendix, pages 144–45.

Dark Quill Gordon (*Ameletus ludens*) don't fly to trees but skitter across the surface and rest on a rock or other debris near the shore. The wings of this particular species are poorly developed because the species is parthenogenic. In other words, the female does not need to mate to lay fertilized eggs, so there is no mating flight.

Finally, the dun changes to a mating adult that scientists call the imago and anglers call the spinner. A very few species like the female White Fly (*Ephoron* spp.) don't change from dun to spinner, but mate as duns. The male White Fly, however, does change to a spinner.

Changing from a dun to a spinner might take the White Fly and Trico a few minutes, but this transformation can take many other species a day or more. Once transformed to a mating adult, male spinners often appear in swarms over faster sections of streams or

Basic nymph patterns

Beadhead Hare's Ear (Olive), Hare's Ear, Flashback Pheasant Tail, Beadhead Pheasant Tail.
For recipes, see Appendix, pages 145–46.

near trees where they have rested. Mated female adults of some of the larger mayflies like the Brown and Green Drake move upstream in huge formations just 10 to 20 feet above the surface. Tricos swarm over faster sections of a stream. Females enter the swarm, mate, and then move upstream to lay their eggs. This is one way species ensure that the entire stream will hold future populations. Upstream eggs move downstream from the water's current.

Females lay their eggs in several ways. Some species like Little Blue-Winged Olive duns actually dive under the surface and scatter their eggs. Other female spinners fall onto the surface and lay their eggs; still others drop their eggs while in flight. The more you

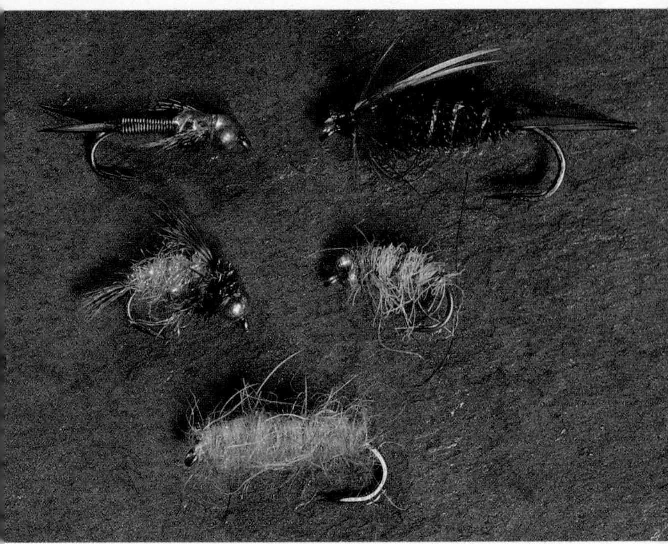

Other nymphs

Copper John, Prince Nymph, Anderson's Bird of Prey Caddis, Standard Beadhead (Caddis Larva), Walt's Worm.
For recipes, see Appendix, pages 146–47.

understand which way each species lays its eggs, the better you'll be prepared to fish the spinnerfall. The best matching-the-hatch events for the fly fisher are those species that drop to the surface and lay their eggs. Because some spinners dive under the surface to lay their eggs, and many spinnners floating on the surface of the water eventually sink, fishing a sinking spinner pattern can work very well during and after spinnerfalls. Eggs hatch in a few weeks to a few months and the mayfly life cycle is completed. The mayfly and stonefly life cycles are termed incomplete life cycles because they lack a fourth stage, the pupa "resting" stage. Caddisfly (Tricoptera) life cycles include this resting stage.

PENNSYLVANIA MAYFLY HATCH CHART

Scientific Name	Common Name
Baetis tricaudatus	Little Blue-Winged Olive, Blue Dun
Epeorus pleuralis	Quill Gordon
Paraleptophlebia adoptiva	Spring Blue Quill, Little Mahogany D
*Siphloplecton basale**	Dark Olive Dun
*Ameletus ludens**	Dark Quill Gordon
Ephemerella subvaria	Hendrickson, Red Quill
Leptophlebia cupida	Black Quill
Acentrella spp.*	Little Blue Dun
Ephemerella invaria	Big Sulphur, Pale Evening Dun
*Leucrocuta aphrodite**	Pale Evening Dun
*Ephemerella septentrionalis**	Pale Evening Dun
Maccaffertium vicarium	March Brown, Gray Fox
Ephemerella dorothea dorothea	Little Sulphur, Pale Evening Dun
Ephemera guttulata	Green Drake
Litobrancha recurvata	Dark Green Drake
Drunella spp.	Blue-Winged Olive
*Siphlonurus quebecensis**	Gray Drake
Isonychia bicolor	Slate Drake
*Maccaffertium ithaca**	Light Cahill
*Serratella deficiens**	Dark Blue Quill
Ephemera simulans	Brown Drake
Stenacron interpunctatum interpunctatum	Light Cahill
*Eurylophella bicolor**	Chocolate Dun
Epeorus vitreus	Pink Cahill, Pink Lady
*Ephemerella needhami**	Olive Sulphur
Paraleptophlebia guttata and *P. mollis*	Summer Blue Quill
Maccaffertium modestum	Cream Cahill
Ephemera varia	Yellow Drake
*Anthopotamus distinctus**	Golden Drake
Tricorythodes spp.	Trico
Leucrocuta hebe	Hebe, Pale Evening Dun
Hexagenia atrocaudata	Big Slate Drake
Ephoron leukon	White Fly

* Minor hatches; Emerges: M = morning, LM = late morning, EA = early afternoon,

Hatch Date	Time of Day	Size
March 1–Apr. 30; Sept. 10–Oct. 30	A (first gen.); E, M (second gen.)	#18–22
Apr. 1–30	EA	#12–14
Apr. 5–30	LM, EA	#16–18
Apr. 5–May 5	A	#12–14
Apr. 10–30	EA	#12–14
Apr. 10–May 10	A	#14–16
Apr. 25–May 15	A	#12–14
May 1–20	A	#20–24
May 5–June 15	E	#14–16
May 5–June 10	LA, E	#16
May 5–June 10	LA, E	#16
May 15–July 15	A, E	#10–14
May 20–June 20	E	#18–20
May 20–June 15	E	#8–12
May 20–June 10	A	#6–10
May 20–July 10	LM, EA	#14–18
May 20–June 10	A	#12–14
May 20–June 30; Sept. 10–Oct. 15	E (first gen.); A (second gen.)	#10–14
May 20–June 15	E	#14
May 20–June 10	E	#18–20
May 21–June 10	E	#10–12
May 25–June 20	EE	#14–16
May 25–June 10	A	#16
May 25–June 30; Sept. 1–Oct. 1	E	#12–16
May 25–June 15	E	#16
June 1–Sept. 30	M	#18–20
June 1–Aug. 30	E	#14–16
June 10–Aug. 10	E	#10–12
June 10–July 10	E	#12
July 10–Oct. 15	M	#22–26
Aug. 5–Oct. 15	A, E	#16–18
Aug. 5–Sept. 1	LE	#6–10
Aug. 10–Sept. 10	E	#12–16

A = afternoon, LA = late afternoon, EE = early evening, E = evening, LE = late evening/night

Little Blue-Winged Olive

JAY NICHOLS PHOTO

Little Blue-Winged Olive dun

(aka *Baetis*, BWO, Blue Dun)
Baetis tricaudatus, prev. *B. vagans*
March 1–April 30 (afternoon); September 10–October 30 (morning/afternoon)
#18–22 (4–7 mm)

Baetis Thorax

Hook:	#18–22 standard dry fly
Thread:	Olive 8/0 Uni-Thread
Tail:	Dun Microfibetts or hackle fibers
Body:	Olive beaver dubbing
Wing:	Blue dun turkey flat
Hackle:	Blue dun

Description

Nymphs: (Swimming) Tan tails (3), tan body and legs with dark brown markings, dark brown wing pads. **Dun:** Gray tails (2) with olive reflections, olive-brown belly and legs, slate backs, and medium slate-gray wings. **Spinner:** Dark grayish-brown tails (2), dark rusty brown body and legs (body has lighter ribbing), and clear wings. Resembles many other *Baetis, Plauditus,* and *Acroneura* species.

Emergence

Sporadic hatches may begin as early as late February, but March and April emergences are more common when forsythia is heavily budded and coltsfoot is just starting to bloom. A second generation of smaller *Baetis* hatches in September and October when fall aster is blooming. In colder weather *Baetis* emerge in the late morning to midafternoon, and during warmer weather they emerge in the morning or near dark.

Behavior and Tactics

Early in the season, dead-drift tannish-olive Hare's Ear Nymphs near vegetation and through riffles. Closer to and during the hatch, the nymphs darken, and are better matched by dead-drifting or slowly stripping Pheasant Tails. *Baetis* nymphs drift or swim in the current until they reach the water's surface. During cold weather, Snowshoe and CDC Burke emergers imitate *Baetis* struggling out of their nymphal shucks trying to take flight. To match the duns, use low-riding dry flies such as parachutes (with white or other highly visible posts), Truform flies, or Comparaduns. If the air temperatures are warmer than usual, the duns are more active and patterns with hackle do a better job of creating the illusion of increased movement. If you are not sure what stage the trout are feeding on, attach a #18-20 Pheasant Tail to your dry fly. Use soft-hackles and sunken spinners to imitate the *Baetis* spinners drifting helplessly in the current after they dive under the surface to lay eggs.

Notes

Prolific in weedy, fertile waters of central and south-central Pennsylvania limestone streams, *Baetis* are one of the most common insects in the state because they are able to colonize a wide range of habitats. This mayfly makes up for its small size with its numbers. *Baetis* sometimes emerge simultaneously with Spring Blue Quills, Quill Gordons, and Hendricksons. In the spring their emergence is particularly tied to Blue Quills. Little Blue-Winged Olives often hatch first, then Spring Blue Quills hatch in equal numbers for an hour or two, until the *Baetis* hatch wanes and only the Spring Blue Quills remain. Days when the water temperature is above 50 degrees but the air temperatures are significantly colder, *Baetis* take a long time to dry their wings and take flights, providing superb fishing.

Premier Hatches

Big Fishing Creek, Delaware River, Falling Springs Branch, Little Juniata River, Little Pine Creek, Spring Creek

Quill Gordon

Quill Gordon dun

Epeorus pleuralis, prev. *Iron fraudator*, *I. pleuralis*
April 1–30 (early afternoon)
#12–14 (9–12 mm)

Quill Gordon

Hook:	#12–14 standard dry fly
Thread:	Olive 8/0 Uni-Thread
Tail:	Dark dun hackle fibers
Body:	Stripped peacock quill
Wing:	Wood duck flank fibers
Hackle:	Dark dun

Description

Nymph: (Clinger) Dark amber tails (2) with dark banding, dark brown body and legs that have areas of amber and heart-shaped markings on the femurs. **Dun:** Dark gray tails (2), dark gray to tannish-gray bodies and tails with olive reflections (body has lighter gray ribbing, and legs have darker heart-shaped markings on the femurs), and slate-gray wings. **Spinner:** Dark brown tails (2), reddish- to tannish-brown body with tannish-cream rib, reddish-brown legs, and clear wings. Resembles *Ameletus ludens*.

Emergence

The first large mayflies of the season usually begin hatching when the forsythia is just about ready to open. Hatches usually commence at the most comfortable time of the day, from about 1 to 2 PM, and generally continue for one or two hours.

Behavior and Tactics

Heavily weighted dark amber to brown Hare's Ears tied to imitate the wide, flat bodies of the naturals and fished with a dead drift through riffles can be effective before the hatch begins. Poor swimmers, the nymphs crawl from fast currents into slow or slack water to emerge, and the same heavily weighted nymphs slowly stripped from faster current toward slack water can be effective. The nymphs usually hold tight to submerged rocks, and emerge on the stream bottom, rising to the surface as fully formed duns. To match this, swing two wets or a wet fly and nymph from fast water into slack water areas. You can weight the flies or just use split-shot on your leader.

After the duns emerge, they often take a long time to dry their substantial wings, because of their subsurface emergence and the cold, raw weather common in April. Duns often stand erect on their legs, a posture best imitated by flies with stiff hackle. Blind-casting dry flies is seldom effective for this hatch, so stalk rising fish. Most of the time the spinnerfalls (commonly fall from 12 to 2 PM) are sparse and do not usually inspire as much feeding activity as the nymphs or duns, though at times fish will feed on them with regularity.

Notes

Epeorus pleuralis received its common angling name "Quill Gordon" because it looks very similar to the Gordon Quill—a dry-fly pattern designed by Theodore Gordon. Mr. Gordon was a Pennsylvania native, born in Pittsburgh, but he became a fly-fishing legend in New York's Catskill Mountain region early in the twentieth century through his extensive writings, and by creating and refining the Catskill style of dry flies.

Intolerant of water pollution, Quill Gordons are only found in the cleanest waters such as the forested freestone waters of the northern tier of the state and the Upper Delaware River. Most Pennsylvania fly anglers view the Quill Gordon only as an early spring hatch. But on some higher altitude streams, like Sixmile Run in northern Centre County, Charlie Meck has found sporadic hatches well into June.

Premier Hatches

Brodhead Creek, Big Fishing Creek, Loyalsock Creek, Sixmile Run, Stony Fork, White Deer Creek, Upper Delaware River

Spring Blue Quill

Spring Blue Quill dun

(aka Paralep, Little Mahogany Dun)
Paraleptophlebia adoptiva
April 5–April 30 (late morning/early afternoon)
#16–18 (6–9 mm)

Weamer's Truform Emerger

Hook:	#16–18 Montana Fly Company 1230
Thread:	Rusty brown 8/0 Uni-Thread
Tail:	Dark brown Darlon
Wing:	Medium dun CDC
Body:	Mahogany beaver dubbing
Post:	Orange Antron
Hackle:	Dark ginger

Description

Nymph: (Crawler) Tails (3) are dark brown nearer body and lighter toward the tips, dark olive-brown body and legs, and dark gray wing pads. **Dun:** Dark grayish-brown tails (3), mahogany to dark brownish-gray body and legs, and slate-gray wings with no markings. **Spinner:** Dark brown tails (3), body, and legs; clear wings. Resembles *Ephemerella deficiens.*

Emergence

This small mayfly appears in large numbers near the beginning of the season when forsythia is heavily budded with some flowers already open and trout lilies are blooming. It is often a concentrated hatch that lasts only a couple hours from late morning until early afternoon. But if it's unusually warm, hatches may continue until evening. Once it begins, expect daily hatches for a week or more.

Behavior and Tactics

Early in the season, olive-brown Hare's Ears dead-drifted through riffles imitate nymphs that are not yet ready to emerge. Nymphs darken before they emerge and Pheasant Tails fished along the edges between fast- and slow-moving water, with a dead drift or slow-stripping retrieve toward shore, imitate naturals that migrate from riffles to slower water and then swim to the surface to shed their nymphal shucks in, or near, the film. Cooler, inclement weather, common in early April, slows the duns from escaping from the surface, and emergers tied with CDC and snowshoe rabbit are effective at this time. As with *Baetis,* use flush-floating dry flies to imitate placidly floating duns and patterns with hackle to imitate duns that are moving more (typical in warmer weather). Spinners fall in the late afternoon or early evening.

Notes

P. adoptiva often emerges with the Little Blue-Winged Olive, Hendrickson, Quill Gordon, and Grannom. Unlike many other Paraleps species, the *adoptiva* male spinner looks similar to the female. In many other Blue Quill species, the male spinner's abdomen becomes clear (it looks similar to a Trico) and is called the Jenny Spinner, but the female is reddish brown.

Premier Hatches

Allegheny River, Bob's Creek, Caldwell Creek, Ninemile Creek, White Deer Creek, Young Woman's Creek

Hendrickson

Hendrickson male dun

Hendrickson female dun

(aka Red Quill,
Light or Dark Hendrickson)
Ephemerella subvaria
April 10–May 10 (afternoon)
#14–16 (9–12 mm)

Snowshoe Emerger

Hook: #12–16 scud
Thread: Pink 8/0 Uni-Thread
Tail: Dark brown Antron
Abdomen: Dark brown beaver dubbing
Rib (optional): Smolt blue Krystal Flash
Wing: Blue dun snowshoe rabbit feet fibers
Thorax: Hendrickson pink beaver dubbing

Description

Nymph: (Crawler) Mottled brown tails (3), brownish-black body and legs with tannish patches, and dark gray wing pads. **Dun:** Dark tannish-gray tails (3) with dark brown band; male has reddish-gray body and legs with lighter ribbing on the body (male) or yellowish-tan body and legs with a pink or olive cast (female); medium gray wings. **Spinner:** Tannish-gray tails (3) with dark brown bands, dark tannish- to reddish-brown legs and body (body has tan ribbing), and clear wings. Males resemble Quill Gordons, but the Hendrickson's belly has pinkish undertones and Quill Gordons only have two tails. Female Hendricksons resemble the Sulphur *E. invaria*.

Emergence

Hendricksons begin hatching sometime around mid-April, when forsythia is fully open, dandelions are blooming, and redbuds are starting to bloom. They continue for about two to three weeks, hatching in the afternoon, often during cold, rainy weather. Warmer weather often produces the best hatches, which also begin in the afternoon but may continue until dark.

Behavior and Tactics

Nymphs are poor swimmers and usually drift freely in faster currents, but they are capable of limited swimming in slower water. Dead-drift brownish-black Hare's Ears or Pheasant Tails (nymphs darken before they emerge) through riffles or slowly strip them toward slack water around in-stream obstructions (like large boulders) and toward the shore.

Hatches can be heaviest near runs at the heads of pools. Colder weather inhibits the hatching duns, and many struggle to escape their nymphal shuck, drifting downstream a long distance while they try to dry their wings. At this time, emergers and dun patterns with trailing shucks work well.

Male and female Hendricksons usually hatch together, and dry flies that have bodies with a pinkish cast usually work fine for both. Sometimes more males than females (or vice versa) will be hatching, and trout may selectively feed on one or the other. Fly patterns tied with grayish-red bodies to imitate the male (#16) and yellowish or pinkish-tan for the female (#14) are necessary when this occurs. Fish the two at the same time to see which one works the best. During particularly warm weather, often when they have been hatching for more than a week, afternoon Hendrickson hatches slow in the late afternoon and then a second wave of duns emerges before dark. Hendricksons provide some of the first reliable evening spinnerfalls of the season. Spinnerfalls are heavily influenced by air temperature and while they usually occur in the early evening, late evening spinnerfalls are common as the hatch progresses.

Notes

Hendricksons live in a wide variety of aquatic habitats. They are one of the most common mayfly species in Pennsylvania and are most widespread in the state's central and northern regions. They received their common angling name from legendary Catskill Mountain (New York) fly fisherman Roy Steenrod who designed a winning dry-fly pattern to imitate this hatch. After several seasons of testing the fly on the Beaverkill River, Steenrod named the fly after his friend and angling companion A. E. Hendrickson.

Hendrickson dun body colors can vary greatly in individual streams, perhaps more so than any other mayfly species. Sample duns from your local waters to find the most effective shade for your imitation. The *Ephemerella subvaria* species is believed to have several subspecies (legendary Pennsylvania angler, Al Caucci, identifies one of them as "Subvaria X"), which have varied coloration and emerge outside the standard time frame for Hendricksons.

Premier Hatches

Allegheny River, Delaware River, Lackawaxen River, Lehigh River, Standing Stone Creek, Tobyhanna Creek

Black Quill

JAY NICHOLS PHOTO

Black Quill dun

Leptophlebia cupida, prev. *Blasturus cupidus*
April 25–May 15 (afternoon)
#12–14, 2XL (9–12 mm)

Weamer's Bucktail Parachute

Hook: #12–14, 2X-long dry fly
Thread: Black 8/0 Uni-Thread
Tail: Three black bucktail hairs
Thorax: Black beaver dubbing
Wing: Dark gray Antron
Abdomen: Three black buck tail hairs, twisted into one strand and wrapped
Hackle: Black

Description

Nymph: (Crawler) Tan tails (3) with dark brown markings; dark brown body, legs, and wing pads. **Dun:** Gray tails (3) with brown bands (the dun's middle tail is shorter than its outer tails); dark slate-gray body with brownish reflections with lighter ribbing; medium slate-gray wings; brownish-black front legs and tan rear legs. **Spinner:** Dark grayish-brown tails (3), dark reddish-brown legs, body with pale yellow ribbing, and clear wings. Resembles *Isonychia bicolor, Ameletus ludens,* and *Epeorus pleuralis.*

Emergence

These large insects usually begin hatching a day or two after the Hendricksons have ended, before the start of the *invaria* Sulphurs. Hatches usually occur in the afternoon, from late April to mid-May, when the apple trees are heavily budded and redbud and dogwood are in bloom.

Behavior and Tactics

Nymphs don't often provide consistent action before or during the hatch, because they are usually found in very shallow water and are generally most active right before dark. But it can be effective to slowly strip black Hare's Ear Nymphs along the shore and in the tails of pools. Nymphs gather in shallow stream sections and collectively migrate upstream, along the shore, often crawling long distances before emergence. Nymphs prefer to emerge into duns in flat, glassy water, where they'll undulate to and from the surface as they try to break out of their nymphal shucks. During warmer weather, fish wet flies tied to imitate the nymphs in the tails of pools and in slack areas near the shore. Let them dangle in the current at the end of the swing to imitate nymphs undulating beneath the surface.

Early May afternoons when the air temperature is abnormally cool, or there is a fine drizzle or mist in the air, usually provide the best opportunity to find trout rising to Black Quills when the inclement weather slows their dun's flight from surface. Dead-drift low-riding dry flies such as parachutes and Comparaduns to rising trout, which will usually be found in the tails of pools. Blind-casting dry flies is seldom effective for this hatch. Spinners (typically fall around noon) are usually more numerous than emerging duns and may provide the best fishing opportunities for this hatch.

Notes

Black Quill nymphs live in slow-moving water with lots of decaying plant material, habitat that isn't prevalent in most of our trout streams. Where they are found, trout eat them, and it's a good idea to keep a few imitations in your boxes if the streams you frequent have even minor populations. You might not encounter a fishable hatch for several seasons, and then one day the necessary conditions align, and you're standing in the middle of trout rising to a Black Quill hatch or spinnerfall.

Premier Hatches

Bald Eagle Creek, Clark Creek, Delaware River, Grays Run, Lost Creek, Penns Creek

Big Sulphur

Big Sulphur dun

(aka Pale Evening Dun)
Ephemerella invaria, prev. *Ephemerella rotunda*
May 5–June 15 (evening)
#14–16 (6–9 mm)

Sparkle Dun

Hook: #14–16 standard dry fly
Thread: Yellow 8/0 Uni-Thread
Tail: Dark brown Antron or Darlon
Body: Yellow beaver dubbing
Wing: Deer hair

Description

Nymph: (Crawler) Buff tails (3), amber to brownish-gray body and legs, and dark gray wing pads. **Dun:** Creamy yellow tails (3), creamy yellow body and legs with an olive cast, and pale to medium gray wings. **Spinner:** Pale cream tails (3), orange-tan body and legs, and clear wings. Resembles many *Heptagenia* species and *Ephemerella septentrionalis*. Female duns look like *E. subvaria*.

Emergence

The hatch begins in early May when lilacs are in bloom and a few days before March Browns begin hatching. Duns often appear in the afternoon for the first few days, but as the hatch progresses (it lasts several weeks), they commonly emerge around 8:30 PM, sometimes coinciding with a spinnerfall. At the end of their emergence for the year, hatches overlap with *E. dorothea dorothea*.

Behavior and Tactics

Most of the year, nymphs are light shades of amber or brown, but they darken significantly before their emergence. Dead-drift amber to light brown Hare's Ears through riffles to imitate the nymphs before they emerge. Fish Pheasant Tails near areas adjacent to slack water—near the shore and around large, in-stream structures like boulders—to imitate nymphs migrating from riffles to slower water to emerge into duns in, or just beneath, the surface film. Often the nymphs struggle to escape their shucks, and they drift helplessly in the current. Patterns with trailing shucks that imitate cripples work well. During cold or rainy weather, flush-riding dry flies work well and in warmer, drier weather, try hackled patterns such as Catskill-style dry flies.

Male spinners gather over riffles at dusk and wait for the females to arrive. After mating, the males often leave the stream before dying, depriving trout the opportunity to eat them. Females also leave the stream, flying to nearby vegetation to wait for their eggs to ripen. But once their eggs are ready, the females return to the water, deposit their eggs, and fall spent to the water's surface. *Invaria* spinners fall in the evening as duns are emerging, making it difficult for anglers to know which stage the trout are eating. At this time, you can cover both stages by fishing a dun and a spinner pattern in tandem.

Notes

The Big Sulphur is one of the most common mayflies in Pennsylvania because it is able to live in a wide variety of aquatic habitats. But the heaviest hatches seem to occur in limestone streams in the central and south-central regions. Duns that appear on the northern freestone streams are a size smaller (#16) than those found in limestone streams.

This species is one of the first mayflies to return to polluted streams, suggesting that *E. invaria* has a higher water-pollution tolerance than most mayflies. Heavy hatches returned to the Little Juniata River and Spring Creek after both began to recover from chemical spills. Many other streams in Pennsylvania's coal mining regions, which are beginning to rehabilitate from acid-mine pollution, also foster Big Sulphur populations. Color and size can vary greatly from stream to stream.

Premier Hatches

Canoe Creek, Codorus Creek, First Fork of the Sinnemahoning, Falling Springs Branch, Letort Spring Run, Spring Creek, Little Juniata River

March Brown

March Brown dun

March Brown spinner

(aka Gray Fox, Great Red Spinner)
Maccaffertium vicarium, prev.
Stenonema vicarium, S. fuscum
May 15–July 15 (afternoon/early evening)
#10–14, 2XL (10–16 mm)

Compara Emerger

Hook:	#10–14 scud
Thread:	Tan 8/0 Uni-Thread
Tail:	Orange Antron
Body:	Light tan beaver dubbing
Wing:	Deer hair

Description

Nymph: (Clinger) Tan to brown tails (3), reddish-brown to dark blackish-brown body with an amber abdomen with darker ribbing, dark brown wing pads, and dark brown legs with some lighter areas. **Dun:** Amber to dark brown tails (2) with darker markings, creamy tan belly with darker brown ribbing on back, pale to tannish-yellow wings are heavily mottled with dark brown to black venations, cream legs with dark brown banding on the femurs. **Spinner:** Dark brown tails (2) with lighter banding, tan body ribbed with dark brown, clear wings with brown venations and a brown area in the front tip, and amber legs with dark brown banding on the femurs. Male spinners have especially large eyes, often colored powdery shades of blue, cream, or light gray. Resembles *Maccaffertium ithaca.*

Emergence

The hatch begins in mid-May, when dame's rocket (pink and white flowers that look like phlox, but phlox has five petals and dame's rocket has four) is just starting to bloom, lilacs have been in bloom for about week, and the Big Sulphur emerges. These large flies emerge during the afternoon and evening for about two weeks, and then slow to a trickle for another week or two. But especially warm weather can trigger morning hatches.

Near the end of the first "March Brown" emergence, smaller, paler versions continue to hatch in the evenings until mid-July. This mayfly used to be called a Gray Fox, but entomologists have determined that they are actually just a continuation of *Maccaffertium vicarium.*

Behavior and Tactics

Nymphs live in swift-moving riffles and glides for most of the year. Dead-drift 2X-long amber or brown Hare's Ears through riffles before the hatch commences for the season. Many tiers create the wide flat shape of the natural in their nymph patterns by squeezing a lead-wire underbody with pliers to flatten it, and then dubbing over the lead. The nymphs often migrate during high-water flows from their fast-water homes to areas of slowed current to emerge into duns in or just below the water's surface. This migration may begin as early as a week before duns first appear on the surface. But if the water is low, then it's common for them to emerge in riffles. During the hatch, slowly strip Beadhead Hare's Ears along the stream bottom toward areas of slack current to imitate naturals preparing to emerge into duns.

Imitate emergers and duns with emerger patterns or flush-floating dry flies dead-drifted to rising trout or blind-cast near pockets of slack water in riffles and runs. Use Catskill-style flies or other patterns with hackle to imitate duns that are aggressively flapping their wings to dry them, common with March Browns.

Spinners often appear in massive numbers, which is hard to believe from the small numbers of duns hatching during the day. But the spinners are actually the combined total from several days' worth of duns. It's common for spinners to hang over riffles at dusk, giving the appearance that they may fall at any second and create a trout feeding frenzy. But then suddenly they are gone, back to the streamside vegetation to wait for another day. Fishing can be fantastic, however, when the spinners do fall to the water.

Notes

March Browns are especially prevalent in streams and rivers with plenty of fast water and rocks. The hatch often comes off in a trickle throughout the day, seldom producing large numbers of flies, but the fish remain focused on the surface, keenly aware of the possibility of one of the flies entering their feeding lane. Because of this, the hatch provides the first opportunity of the season to blind-cast dry flies through riffles, runs, and other places that look like they hold fish.

Premier Hatches

Bald Eagle Creek, Big Fill Run, Delaware River, Penns Creek, Pine Creek, Piney Creek

Little Sulphur

(aka Pale Evening Dun, Pale Watery Dun, Summer Sulphur)
Ephemerella dorothea dorothea, prev. *Ephemerella dorothea*
May 20–June 20 (evening)
#18–20 (5–8 mm)

Meck's Vernille Parachute

Hook: #18–20 standard dry fly
Thread: Light cahill 8/0 Uni-Thread
Body: Yellow Vernille
Wing: Light gray Antron
Hackle: Cream

Description

Nymph: (Crawler) Pale olive tails (3) with dark brown markings, dark brown body with amber areas, dark brown mottled wing pads, pale olive legs with dark brown markings. **Dun:** Cream tails (3), pale creamish-yellow to orange body with olive reflections, pale gray wings, pale yellowish-cream legs. **Spinner:** Cream tails (3), creamish-yellow body, glassy clear wings, and pale cream legs. Resembles *Ephemerella invaria, Ephemerella septentrionalis, Leucrocuta Aphrodite,* and *Leucrocuta hebe.*

Emergence

Little Sulphurs usually begin hatching during evenings in late May when rhododendron flowers are opening and mountain laurel is in bloom. They continue for several weeks until mid-June, overlapping with other mayfly species, including Green Drakes, but trout seem to prefer Sulphurs.

Behavior and Tactics

Before the hatch begins, dead-drift Beadhead Pheasant Tails through riffles or suspend them beneath a large dry fly in slow-moving pools. Poor swimmers that live in nearly all types of aquatic habitat—from slow pools to riffles—the nymphs can emerge into duns in the surface film, but they mainly float just under the surface, wiggling out of their nymphal shucks. To imitate this, fish unweighted Pheasant Tails, greased and fished in the film, with a dead drift and an occasional twitch to bulging fish (fish that are eating with boiling rises just beneath the surface).

The heaviest hatches most commonly occur at dusk or dark and bring many trout to the surface. Dead-drift emerger patterns and flush-floating dry-fly patterns to steadily rising trout. Once *E. dorothea dorothea* has been hatching for a few days, spinners fall at the same time duns are hatching. When this happens, try a dun imitation first, because they are easier to see in low light. At times, however, the trout will feed selectively on spent wing patterns.

Notes

In some tailwater fisheries, like the Upper Delaware River, *E. dorothea dorothea* produces more than one generation per year. This must be caused by the artificially cold temperatures created by the dam's water releases. Hatches on the Upper Delaware can last as long as three months, but the size of the duns decreases as the hatch progresses. Little Sulphurs commonly have wide variations in body color, depending on the stream and what the nymphs ate.

Little Sulphurs do not reside in as many streams as Big Sulphurs (*Ephemerella invaria*), but they are still fairly common throughout the state.

Premier Hatches

Brodhead Creek, Delaware River, Driftwood Branch of the Sinnemahoning Creek, Kettle Creek, Little Bald Eagle Creek, Pine Creek

Green Drake

Green Drake dun

Green Drake spinner

(aka Shad Fly, Coffin Fly)
Ephemera guttulata
May 20–June 15 (evening)
#8–12, 2XL (16–26mm)

Weamer's Comparachute

Hook: #8–12 Daiichi 1230
Thread: Light cahill 8/0 Uni-Thread
Tail: Dark brown Darlon
Body: Pale yellow beaver dubbing
Wing: Olive deer hair
Hackle Post: Cream Antron
Hackle: Grizzly dyed olive

Description

Nymph: (Burrower) Tannish-brown tails (3), tan body, dark brown wing pads, and tan legs with darker markings. **Dun:** Dark brownish-black tails (3), pale yellowish-cream body, yellowish-green wings with black venations; dark brown front legs and cream rear legs. Male duns are often much smaller (two sizes) than the female. **Spinner:** Tails (3) have dark brown bands, chalky white body, clear wings (sometimes with a yellow cast) with prominent black venations; front legs are dark brown and back pairs are cream. Resembles *Litobrancha recurvata, Ephemera varia, Hexagenia rigida*.

Emergence

Green Drake duns hatch around Memorial Day, when the white flowers on black locusts are almost fully open. Sensitive to light, they often begin hatching in the last hour before dark. On cloudy days or on streams shaded during the day by mountains or heavy tree canopy hatches can begin in the afternoon and continue into darkness.

Behavior and Tactics

Nymphs burrow into fine gravel and sandy areas in the streambed. When they leave their underground homes to feed or emerge, they become vulnerable to trout. Before the hatch begins, dead-drift or slowly strip large, heavily weighted, 2X-long tan Hare's Ears through riffles. Green Drake nymphs swim to the surface to molt into duns, wiggling up and down at or just beneath the surface as they try to shed their nymphal skins. This struggling movement is irresistible to trout but difficult to imitate with fly patterns. Try fishing an unweighted or lightly weighted Hare's Ear or wiggle nymph with short, quick strips or swinging the fly in the current, allowing it to dangle at the end of your presentation so the flowing water moves the fly and mimics the natural's up-and-down motions.

Many anglers leave the stream too early and then complain that this hatch is overhyped. It's common, especially during warm weather, for duns to emerge in large numbers only after dark. Early on, the duns are best imitated with large dry flies that have dark brown trailing shucks. But after they have been emerging for more than a couple of days, trout tend to prefer duns that move (at least during the day). It's difficult to mimic the way that the large Green Drakes flutter their wings to dry them, and trout can easily discern a forgery. A high-riding Catskill-style pattern gently twitched about a foot in front of a rising trout and then fished drag-free over the fish sometimes works well.

The peak of the hatch, and sometimes the best fishing, occurs during the spinnerfall. About an hour before dark, the spinners usually flutter in and out of the treetops—in such staggering numbers on some rivers that you can hear their wings clicking as they fly. As darkness approaches, massive waves of Green Drakes fly upstream looking for mates. After mating, the males die and fall spent to the water. The females deposit their eggs, and also fall spent.

The intense spinnerfalls cause two major problems for anglers. First, this extreme biomass of food on the water often makes it difficult to get trout to notice your fly. Second, because much of the action takes place after dark, it is hard to see your fly to determine whether you are casting accurately or if a fish has taken your fly. Using an easy-to-see pattern such as a #4–6 Hi-Vis White Wulff or a Dette Coffin Fly (tied on 2X-long hooks) helps solve both of these problems. These oversized patterns are easier for the fish to see and you can also track them in the moonlight. Cut back your tippet to 3X or 4X to prevent the larger flies from twisting your tippets and to give you the extra strength for landing the larger trout that feed after dark.

Notes

The nymphs have a two-year life cycle, so the duns that emerge this year have hatched from eggs that were deposited two seasons ago. Hatches are more frequent across the northern tier and central Pennsylvania than they are in the southern part of the state. The common angling name for the Green Drake spinner, the Coffin Fly, was created by Catskill Mountain (New York) fly-fishing legends Walt Dette and Ted Townsend. They coined the name while tying flies after a funeral to imitate the chalky white spinners.

Sulphurs often emerge at the same time as Green Drakes, and trout seem to have a preference for this smaller fly. Study a rising fish closely to determine if they are eating Sulphurs or Drakes. But even if the fish you are casting to is obviously eating Green Drakes, it's a good idea to show it a Sulphur pattern if it has refused your Drakes. Slate Drakes also often appear at the same time as Green Drakes an hour or two earlier in the evening.

Size varies greatly from stream to stream, though they are generally larger on limestone streams than freestone streams. No matter where they live, males are usually one to two sizes smaller than females.

Premier Hatches

Big Fishing Creek, Cedar Run, Delaware River, East Hickory Creek, Penns Creek, Yellow Creek

Dark Green Drake

Litobrancha recurvata, prev. *Hexagenia recurvata*
May 20–June 10 (afternoon)
#6–10, 2XL (20–28 mm)

Deer Hair Parachute

Hook:	#6–10, 2X-long dry fly
Thread:	Olive 8/0 Uni-Thread
Tail:	Deer hair
Body:	Dark olive beaver dubbing
Wing:	Deer hair
Hackle:	Grizzly dyed dark olive

Description

Nymph: (Burrower) Tails (3) brown outer and cream middle, red-brown back/legs, brown wing pads, olive-brown feathery gills. **Dun:** Long black tails (2) with a miniscule, vestigial third tail between them, dark slate-gray body ribbed with yellow, dark gray wings with olive-green reflections, dark brown front legs and tan rear legs. **Spinner:** Brown tails (2), orange-tan body/legs, pale wings with brown venations. Resembles *Ephemera guttulata.*

Emergence

Duns hatch in late May when the rhododendrons are just opening, usually from about 1 to 3 PM, and they continue hatching for a week or more.

Behavior and Tactics

Nymphs and duns behave just like Green Drakes, so fish Dark Green Drake imitations in a similar manner (see pages 52–55). Spinners usually fall at dusk and can be heavy if cold weather forces several days' worth of spinners to fall in the same evening. It's easier to catch fish during Dark Green Drake spinnerfalls than it is during Green Drake spinnerfalls because, usually, there are fewer naturals on the water. Fish high-riding patterns like Gray Wulffs tied with white or fluorescent-colored wings that you and the trout can see well.

Notes

Look for Dark Green Drakes on fertile streams with sandy or silt-bottomed areas in the central and south-western regions of the state. Because duns are so large, and often emerge in early afternoon, they usually live in small streams with tight, heavy canopies. The vegetation allows them to hide from predators quickly after hatching. Like *Ephemera guttulata,* nymphs have a two-year life cycle, and the duns that emerge this year have hatched from eggs that were deposited two seasons ago.

Often Dark Green Drakes and Green Drakes appear concurrently. Though they appear similar to Green Drakes, the two species are unrelated. Dark Green Drakes have only two long tails with a miniscule, vestigial third tail between them (the vestigial tail is a common characteristic of *Hexagenia,* a genus that once included the Dark Green Drake). Green Drakes have three equally long tails. Also, Dark Green Drakes have dark-colored bellies, but Green Drake bellies are light-colored.

Premier Hatches

Big Fill Run, Elk Creek, Garner Run, Little Mahoning Creek, Little Sandy Creek, Vanscoyoc Run

Blue-Winged Olive

Blue-Winged Olive dun

(aka BWO, Cornuta)
Drunella lata, D. cornuta, D. cornutella
May 20–July 10 (late morning/early afternoon)
#14–18 (7–12 mm)

CDC Biot Comparadun

Hook:	#14–18 standard dry fly
Thread:	Green 8/0 Uni-Thread
Tail:	Medium dun Microfibetts
Abdomen:	Green turkey biots
Wing:	Blue dun CDC
Thorax:	Green beaver dubbing

Description

Nymph: (Crawler) Brown tails (3) lighter at the tips, brown body with lighter ribbing, mottled brown wing pads, and medium brown legs. **Dun:** Pale gray-olive tails (3), bright chartreuse to medium olive body, medium to dark slate-gray wings, amber-olive legs. **Spinner:** Dark gray tails (3), blackish-olive body; clear wings, dark olive-brown legs. Resembles *Drunella attenuata, Drunella walkeri,* and *Ephemerella needhami* (female).

Emergence

Hatches begin in late May when peonies are opening and continue on many streams into late June or early July. Some members of this species appear in limited numbers on some streams well into August or even September. Emergences occur late morning and early afternoon, though weather can influence this timing.

Behavior and Tactics

Dead-drift weighted Pheasant Tails through riffles, or slowly strip them from fast water to slack water to match nymphs preparing to emerge. Even though they live in riffles and sections of streams with current, the nymphs are poor swimmers, so they migrate to calmer water to emerge in, or below, the surface. Unweighted Pheasant Tails greased and cast to rising fish, or slowly twitched and stripped below the surface, imitate nymphs emerging into duns.

Brightly colored when they first emerge, duns darken quickly when exposed to air. They often escape from the surface quickly, so evening spinnerfalls sometimes produce better fly-fishing opportunities than the hatch. If you hit this hatch on a cool, overcast, or drizzly day, the duns will stay on the water longer as they dry their wings, and trout will feed heavily on emergers and duns. Patterns tied with with bright chartreuse bodies imitate the color of newly hatched *D. lata.* Trout feed heavily on *D. lata* spinnerfalls, so be prepared with patterns with exaggerated thoraxes to imitate the spinners' unusually robust olive-black bodies.

Notes

Differentiating between *Drunella cornuta, D. cornutella,* and *D. lata* has created a lot of confusion. Entomologists have now reversed their decision to combine all three species into *D. lata* and again consider these insects to be three separate species, maintaining their previous taxonomical designations. These three Blue-Winged Olives species may be found hatching for most of the season, though the size of the insects decreases as the months progress.

Because these mayflies hatch from late spring until late summer, weather can have a dramatic effect on the timing of the emergence and spinnerfall. Typical hatches begin in late morning, and they continue for an hour or two. But extremely warm weather can cause a hatch to occur earlier in the morning. Especially cool weather can delay an emergence until after 12 PM. Weather can also affect the spinnerfall, which occurs in the evening after 7 PM. If the weather is warm, spinners often won't reach the water until after dark or early the next morning.

Premier Hatches

Big Fishing Creek, Elk Creek, Honey Creek, Kettle Creek, Little Juniata River, Penns Creek

Slate Drake

Slate Drake dun

Slate Drake spinner

(aka Leadwing Coachman, White-Gloved Howdy, Iso)
Isonychia bicolor, prev. *Isonychia harperi, I. matilda, I. albomanicata, I. sadleri*
May 20–June 30 (evening); September 10–October 15 (afternoon)
#10–14, 2XL (12–18 mm)

Weamer's Burke Emerger

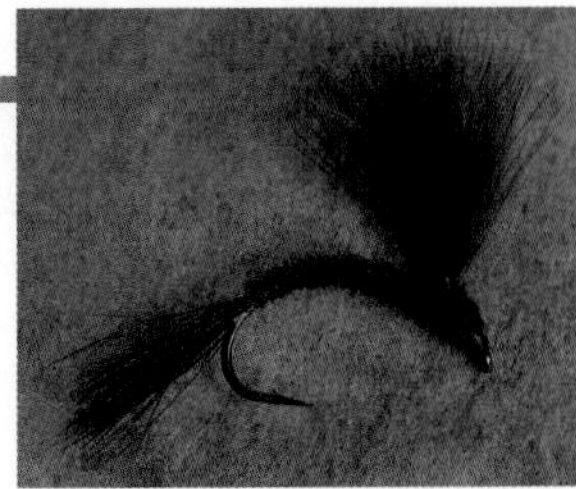

Hook: #10–14 scud
Thread: Olive 8/0 Uni-Thread
Tail: Mink guard hairs
Body: Maroon beaver dubbing
Wing: Medium dun CDC

Description

Nymph: (Swimming) Dark gray tails (3), brownish-black body with a lighter lateral stripe on the top, dark gray wing pads, pale olive-gray legs. **Dun:** Medium brownish-gray tails (2), reddish-mahogany or dark slate-gray body with olive reflections (depending on the stream); front legs match body color, rear legs are cream. **Spinner:** Medium gray tails (2), dark reddish-mahogany body, clear wings, rear two pairs of legs are cream and front pair is dark brown. Resembles Dark Quill Gordon (*Ameletus ludens*) and Gray Drake (*Siphlonurus quebecensis*).

Emergence

Isonychia bicolor produces two generations each year. The first generation emerges from late May through June, when mountain laurel is blooming and oxeye daisy is beginning to bloom. The second generation appears in September and October when aster is blooming. It's also common to find a few *Isonychia* hatching throughout the summer months, particularly during cool or rainy weather. Hatches often begin around 7 PM during warm weather in the late spring. Afternoon hatches are common during the cooler weather that often accompanies the second generation. It's not uncommon to see March Browns spinners when the first generation appears and Little Blue-Winged Olives with the second.

Behavior and Tactics

To imitate the great swimming ability of the nymphs, strip Prince Nymphs or Pheasant Tails through riffles toward the shore with short, quick tugs on the fly line or cast weighted wet flies tied with peacock-herl bodies and reddish-brown hackle collars into fast water and retrieve them toward shore with the same stripping techniques. Use 4X tippets because fish can strike violently.

Nymphs live in fast water, but swim or crawl to rocks and debris along the shore to emerge. Not all hatched duns will be accessible to the trout unless they are blown back into the stream by the wind. But some duns also emerge in-stream when the water is high or if they have hatched from deep runs. These duns float downstream while they attempt to dry their wings, making Iso dry flies and emergers effective patterns. It's uncommon to find a lot of *Isonychia* duns on the surface, but trout seem to be on the lookout for those that hatch in-stream, making *Isonychia* dry flies and emergers super searching patterns from late spring through fall.

Springtime spinnerfalls usually occur at dusk, but they may be found in the afternoon during cool weather. Afternoon falls are also common during their second generation in the autumn. The spinners can provide excellent dry-fly opportunities, but *Isonychia* spinners are particularly sensitive to weather, much like March Browns, and it's common for them to retreat to streamside vegetation if the conditions aren't quite right. Imitate evening *Isonychia* spinners with Truform or Antron spinner patterns. For afternoon spinners, sparse hackle-wing spinners or Stroup CDC Spinners may be better choices.

Notes

A good indication that the hatch has begun is the black nymphal shucks on rocks along the edges of the stream. The number of shucks will indicate how intense the hatch has been. Size varies from generation to generation and stream to stream. Duns produced during the first generation, May through June, are larger (#10–12) than the duns in the second generation, September through October (#12–14). Body color also varies. Some freshly emerged duns can have a bright green or olive coloration to their bodies—it's very important to have a few emerger patterns tied with these body colors. The flies darken when they are exposed to air, so trout rising to the duns may be taking different colored flies than those rising to emergers.

Generally, the second generation produces better fishing opportunities than the first. Few other insects are on the water in September and October to compete for the trout's attention.

Premier Hatches

Delaware River, Lehigh River, Little Juniata River, Little Pine Creek, Loyalsock Creek, Penns Creek

Brown Drake

Brown Drake dun

Ephemera simulans
May 21–June 10 (evening)
#10–12, 2XL (11–18 mm)

Antron Parachute Emerger

Hook: #10–12, 2X-long dry fly
Thread: Olive 8/0 Uni-Thread
Tail: Dark brown Darlon
Body: Light olive beaver dubbing
Wing: Dark brown Darlon
Hackle: Grizzly dyed olive

Description

Nymph: (Burrower) Tan tails (3), tannish-gray body, dark brown mottled wing pads, and tan legs. **Dun:** Dark brown tails (3) banded with tan, tannish-yellow, or olive, belly and legs with dark brown markings, brown back, olive yellowish-tan wings and hind wing heavily spotted with dark brown. **Spinner:** Tails (3) tan with dark brown bands, tannish-yellow body with dark brown markings, clear wings heavily barred with dark brown markings, dark brown front legs and rear legs that are cream with dark brown tips. Resembles March Brown *Maccaffertium vicarium*. But March Browns are usually a bit smaller, lighter in color, and have two tails. Spinners resemble *Hexagenia atrocaudata* spinners, but the latter is larger and has two tails rather than three. (*Hexagenia* has a vestigial middle tail.)

Emergence

Brown Drakes hatch sometime around May 20 when peonies are in full bloom and the flowers on the black locust trees are almost fully open. Like Green Drakes, Brown Drakes are sensitive to light and emerge at dusk or later, but on cloudy days or on streams shaded during the day by mountains or heavy tree canopy, hatches can begin in the afternoon.

Behavior and Tactics

Brown Drake nymphs prefer to live in slow to moderate currents where they burrow into fine to fairly coarse streambed substrate. Large, heavily weighted, 2X-long tannish-gray Hare's Ears will catch fish if they are dead-drifted or slowly stripped along the streambed in the braided water below riffles before the hatch begins. Brown Drake nymphs swim to the surface with an up-and-down undulating motion like Green Drakes, where they emerge at, or just below, the surface. Fish the imitations in a similar manner to Green Drakes (see pages 52–55).

Male spinners begin their mating flight near trees around 7 PM. Female spinners, after mating, fly toward the surface and travel upstream. More than any other mayfly species, Brown Drake duns and spinners are concentrated for only a few days on a stream, making spectacular spinnerfalls common. Often, your fly patterns will have to compete with thousands of naturals for the trout's attention. Try using oversized flies (one to two sizes larger than the natural) to get the trout's attention and help you spot your pattern, sink your dun or spinner a few inches beneath the surface, or use spinner patterns with upright wings—Brown Drake spinners have the unusual tendency of floating with their wings held upright after mating. You can also fish a spinner pattern behind a highly visible dun imitation.

Notes

Brown Drakes live mainly in large, northern waters that flow north to south. Heaviest concentrations are from the Delaware River on the eastern border to Neshannock Creek, just southeast of Mercer, in the west. Brown Drakes mainly inhabitant freestone streams in Pennsylvania, but they do live in one limestone stream, Honey Creek. Brown Drakes begin emerging near the end of the Green Drake hatch in rivers and streams where they cohabitate. The number of Brown Drake duns compared to Green Drake duns is a good indicator of how much longer the Green Drakes will continue to hatch.

Premier Hatches

Cool Spring, Little Mahoning Creek, Kettle Creek, Neshannock Creek, Pine Creek, Raystown Branch of the Juniata River, Delaware River

Light Cahill

Stenacron interpunctatum interpunctatum, prev. *Stenonema canadense, Stenacron canadense, S. interpunctatum, S. heterotarsale*
May 25–June 20 (early evening)
#14–16 (9–12 mm)

Light Cahill (Catskill Style)

Hook:	#14–16 standard dry fly
Thread:	Light cahill 8/0 Uni-Thread
Tail:	Cream hackle fibers
Body:	Creamish-tan beaver dubbing
Wing:	Wood duck
Hackle:	Cream

Description

Nymph: (Clinger) Medium to dark brown tails (3), dark brown body with some lighter areas, mottled brown wing pads, and tan legs with darker areas. **Dun:** Creamish-yellow tails (2), orangish-yellow (female) or creamy yellow (male) body, often with olive reflections; pale yellow wings with barring; and creamish-yellow legs with dark brown barring. **Spinner:** Creamish-yellow tails (2) with dark brown banding and creamish-yellow body (the female's abdomen has a distinct orange cast from the eggs), and glassy clear wings. Resembles *Epeorus vitreus* (female only).

Emergence

A few Light Cahill duns may begin to appear as early as the end of May. But the hatch isn't usually significant until early June, when oxeye daisies and mountain laurel are blooming. By the end of June, the Light Cahill hatch has normally ended for the season. Emergences usually occur in evening, beginning around 7 PM. Light Cahills often appear with Green Drakes and an hour or two before Sulphurs, so be prepared to fish both hatches.

Behavior and Tactics

Nymphs are clingers and share the same wide, flat-shape body as March Browns. Dead-drift tannish-brown Hare's Ears through riffles and runs before the hatch begins. Nymphs migrate to slower stream sections, often near the middle and tails of pools, where they drift or swim to just below the surface to emerge into duns.

Standard dry flies, tied without trailing shucks, such as Comparaduns and parachutes, will catch fish that are rising to duns—trailing shucks are unnecessary because the nymphs emerge into duns below the surface. Light Cahills hatch when the light is low, and high-riding Catskill-style dries and Blonde Wulffs are easier to see. Light Cahill spinnerfalls create some of the best dry-fly fishing opportunities for this species.

Notes

Though many entomologists write that this mayfly can only survive in clean, unspoiled waters, Meck has found specimens of *S. interpunctatum interpunctatum* in several streams that are recovering from man-made aquatic insect kills, before other mayfly species returned. This species is particularly abundant on some of central

Pennsylvania's larger limestone streams. Coloration varies greatly from stream to stream.

Premier Hatches

Blacklog Creek, Delaware River, Frankstown Branch of the Juniata River, Little Juniata River, Penns Creek, Spring Creek

Pink Cahill

Pink Cahill dun

(aka Vitreus; males, Light Cahill; females, Pink Lady)
Epeorus vitreus, prev. *Epeorus humeralis*, *Iron humeralis*
May 25–June 30; September 1–October 1 (evening)
#12–16 (8–12 mm)

Para-Scud

Hook:	#12–16 scud
Thread:	Olive 8/0 Uni-Thread
Abdomen:	Orange beaver dubbing
Wing:	Blue dun Antron
Hackle:	Grizzly dyed light olive
Thorax:	Light olive beaver dubbing

Description

Nymph: (Clinger) Dark brown tails (2), amber bodies underneath with a dark area near the tail and on the dorsal part of the body, dark brown mottled wing pads, tan legs with darker heart-shaped markings on the femurs. **Dun:** Dark grayish-brown tails (2), pale olive thorax; pinkish-cream to orange (female) or pale yellow to pale olive (male) abdomen. Both have darker reddish markings on back; pale gray to gray wings, sometimes with a yellow cast or olive reflections; creamish-yellow or olive legs banded with dark brown heart-shaped markings on the femurs. **Spinner:** Creamish-tan tails (2), pinkish-red (female) or dark olive (male) body, clear wings, creamish-tan legs barred with darker heart-shaped markings on the femurs. Resembles *Stenacron interpunctatum interpunctatum*; females look like *Ephemerella invaria*; males look like *Epeorus pleuralis.*

Emergence

Epeorus vitreus begins its initial emergence at the end of May or the beginning of June when mountain laurel is blooming and oxeye daisies are just starting to bloom. Hatches continue through July. A second generation, approximately one size smaller, hatches in September when the aster is blooming. *Vitreus* hatches commence in the early evening and they can continue until dark.

Behavior and Tactics

Dead-drift dark amber to brown Hare's Ears (tied wide and flat) through riffles before the hatch begins. Nymphs are poor swimmers, so they crawl from fast currents into slow or slack water to emerge. To imitate the migrating nymphs, try stripping patterns heavily weighted with tungsten beads or extra split-shot from faster currents toward slack water. Nymphs usually hold tight to submerged rocks and emerge on the stream bottom, rising to the surface as fully formed duns. Match this by swinging weighted wet flies or a wet and a nymph from fast water into slack areas.

Duns seldom spend much time on the water after emerging, so it's uncommon to have large numbers of trout feeding on them. A Para-Scud is a good imitation of a dun breaking through the surface film. *E. vitreus* duns often stand erect on their legs for brief moments before they fly, a posture best imitated by stiff-hackled Catskill fly patterns. Occasionally twitching or skittering these patterns to sporadically rising trout will elicit a strike.

Spinnerfalls usually occur in the evening or at dusk. But they may be delayed until early the next morning during especially warm weather. Though there is a distinct color difference between the males or females, trout seldom become selective to either of them. Dark olive or pinkish-red spinners will both catch fish.

Notes

E. vitreus, like *E. pleuralis* (Quill Gordon), is intolerant of water pollution and is only found in Pennsylvania's purest trout waters. Male and female duns have distinct color differences that are magnified when the duns transform into spinners. The females turn a deep pinkish red, the color of salmon fillets, prompting some anglers to call them Salmon Spinners.

It is not a widely recognized or scientifically proven fact that *vitreous* produces two generations per year. But based on our observations and stream samplings, we believe they do. Slate Drakes appear with the first and second generations.

Premier Hatches

Big Fishing Creek, Brodhead Creek, Delaware River, Fishing Creek (Columbia County), Sixmile Run, Young Woman's Creek

Summer Blue Quill

Summer Blue Quill dun

(aka Paralep, Blue Dun, Little Mahogany Dun)
Paraleptophlebia mollis, P. guttata
June 1–September 30 (morning)
#18–20 (6–9 mm)

Blue Dun

Hook: #18–20 standard dry fly
Thread: Gray 8/0 Uni-Thread
Tail: Light dun hackle fibers
Body: Gray Super Fine dubbing
Wings: Light dun hen-hackle tips
Hackle: Light dun

Description

Nymph: (Crawler) Dark brown tails (3) that are lighter in toward the tips, dark gray wing pads, dark olive-brown to black body and legs. **Dun:** Dark grayish-brown tails (3), dark gray body, grayish-tan legs, and slate-gray wings. **Spinner:** Dark brown tails (3); dark brown body (female) or hyaline abdomen with the last few segments dark brown (male); dark brown legs, and clear wings. Male duns resemble *Ephemerella deficiens* and male spinners resemble Trico spinners.

Emergence

Summer Blue Quills hatch almost every morning throughout the summer, at the same time as milkweed is in full bloom. Hatches can be important when the weather is unusually cool or inclement and the newly emerged duns can't readily take flight. Look for the hatch to appear on a cool, inclement summer morning, often as early as 6 AM.

Behavior and Tactics

Fish dark Pheasant Tails or Turkey Tail Nymphs in the slower water next to riffles and move them from the faster to slower water to imitate the nymphs migrating from riffles. Nymphs shed their shucks in the surface film.

Notes

Many of Pennsylvania's better limestone streams have great hatches from late June through much of September. The spinners appear in the air about the same time as Tricos. Summer Blue Quill spinners fly up and down, whereas Tricos move more horizontally.

Premier Hatches

Elk Creek, Spruce Creek, Little Juniata River, Cedar Run, Penns Creek, Upper Delaware River

Cream Cahill

Maccaffertium modestum, prev. *Stenonema modestum*
June 1–August 30 (evening)
#14–16 (9–12 mm)

Usual

Hook: #14–16 Daiichi 1170 or 1180
Thread: Light cahill 8/0 Uni-Thread
Tail: Cream snowshoe rabbit feet fibers
Body: Cream beaver dubbing
Wing: Cream snowshoe rabbit feet fibers

Description

Nymph: (Clinger) Pale gray tails (3), pale gray body and wing pads, cream legs. **Dun:** Cream tails (2), pale cream body, and cream wings and legs. **Spinner:** Cream tails (2), cream (if it still has eggs in it) or white (if eggs are exuded) body, clear wings, white to pale cream legs. Resembles White Fly (*Ephoron leukon*).

Emergence

Cream Cahills share many of the same physical traits and emergence characteristics as March Browns—they are both part of the *Maccaffertium* genus. Cream Cahills hatch in the evening from early June when oxeye daisies, mountain laurel, and milkweed are blooming through early September.

Behavior and Tactics

Dead-drift pale gray Hare's Ears through riffles before and during the hatch. Tie these flies wide and flat, just like those described in the March Brown section, to imitate the distinct body shape of these flat-bodied clingers that live in swift-moving riffles and glides for most of the year. They emerge into duns in or just below the water's surface. Cream Cahills usually hatch in the early evening from 6 to 8 PM. Emerger patterns are not so effective because they are hard to see this late in the day and trout will usually show little preference between emergers and the easier-to-see dun patterns. Hatches are not often heavy or concentrated, but the spinnerfalls at dusk can be heavy and provide the best dry-fly fishing opportunities. Catskill- and Wulff-style flies are good choices for spinner imitations because they are easy for you, and the fish, to see as darkness approaches—important during heavy spinnerfalls. These hackled flies also imitate female spinners hovering above and briefly touching the water to release their eggs.

Notes

Cream Cahills hatch on larger streams across the central and southern parts of the state. Because they can hatch in mid- and late summer, anglers often confuse them with White Flies. But unlike White Flies, Cream Cahills fly farther above the surface when it emerges and when it mates. All Cream Cahills have two tails; male White Flies have three.

Premier Hatches

Cross Fork Creek, French Creek, Kettle Creek, Little Juniata River, Lycoming Creek, Octoraro Creek

Yellow Drake

Yellow Drake dun

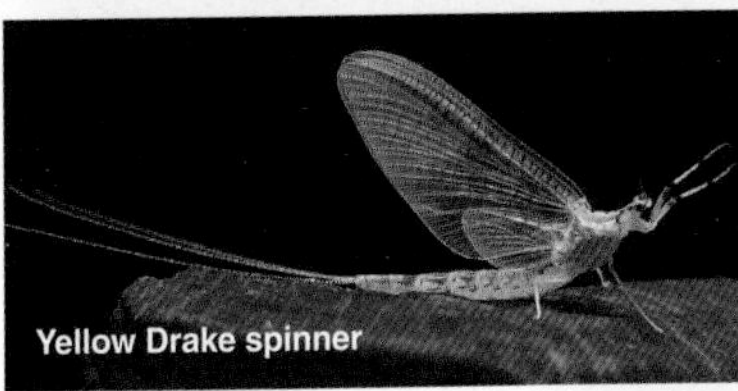
Yellow Drake spinner

Ephemera varia
June 10–August 10 (evening)
#10–12, 2XL (12–14 mm)

Comparadun

Hook:	#10–12, 2X-long dry fly
Thread:	Light cahill 8/0 Uni-Thread
Tail:	Medium dun Microfibetts
Body:	Pale yellow beaver dubbing
Wing:	Deer hair

Description

Nymph: (Burrower) Pale gray tails (3), amber body with darker markings, medium brown mottled wing pads, and creamish-tan legs. **Dun:** Tan tails (3) with darker markings, pale yellow body with brown markings on its belly that look like quotation marks; pale yellow wings with brown venations (hind wing has no venations);

pale yellow legs, front pair with darker markings. **Spinner:** Creamish-yellow tails (3) banded with dark brown; creamish-yellow body with dark brown lines, especially on last four segments; clear wings; rear two pairs of legs are creamish-yellow and front legs are tannish-yellow with darker markings. Yellow Drake duns look nearly identical to the spinners. The only difference is that spinners' wings are clear. Resembles *Hexagenia rigida* and *Ephemera guttulata.*

Emergence

Yellow Drakes begin emerging in mid-June when elderberry and chicory are just blooming. This hatch is especially long-lived, and occasional stragglers may emerge into August. The duns appear just before dark around 8:45 PM, and continue hatching for approximately a half hour.

Behavior and Tactics

Yellow Drake nymphs are burrowers that prefer to live in warmer, slower sections of streams. Prior to hatching, they leave their burrows and undulate toward the surface to emerge in the film. Imitate this behavior by fishing amber 2X-long and brown Hare's Ear with the same tactics as for the Green Drake nymph (pages 52–55).

Yellow Drakes seldom hatch in large numbers—and trout sometimes ignore them—but the duns quivering on the surface as they attempt to dry their wings can bring on aggressive rises from trout. Try skittering hackled flies in front of a rising trout to imitate this. Duns and spinners are on the water in the dark and large (#8–10) Comparaduns tied with white or bleached hair, Catskill-style patterns, and Hi-Vis Wulffs are easier to see. Use 4X so the large flies don't twist your tippet and you have extra strength for landing the larger trout that feed after dark. Spinners appear at dusk, but seldom fall spent to the water until after dark, after most anglers have gone home.

Notes

Yellow Drakes prefer to live in warmer and slower water than Brown or Green Drakes. And since Yellow Drakes never emerge in mind-boggling numbers like the other drakes, they seldom create the same intense trout fishing opportunities. Most trout have left the warmer sections of streams by the time Yellow Drakes begin to emerge, but you may find good numbers of rising fish if the weather has been cool. If you find yourself streamside without a Yellow Drake fly pattern during a hatch, a size 10 or 12 Light Cahill usually works just as well.

Premier Hatches

Bald Eagle Creek, Blacklog Creek, Bowman Creek, Fishing Creek (Columbia County), Little Juniata River, Little Bald Eagle Creek

Trico

Trico dun

Tricorythodes spp., prev. *Tricorythus* spp.
July 10–October 15 (morning)
#22–26 (3–4 mm)

Antron Spinner

Hook: #22–26 standard dry fly
Thread: Black 8/0 Uni-Thread
Tail: Light dun Microfibetts
Abdomen: Black thread or beaver dubbing
Wing: White Antron
Thorax: Black beaver dubbing

Description

Nymph: (Crawler) Tan tails (3), dark brown body with lighter coloration toward the rear; dark brown, mottled wing pads; tan legs. **Dun:** Three cream tails, body is pale to medium olive (female) or dark brown (male); pale gray forewings (no hind wing); pale cream legs. **Spinner:** Short cream tails (3) the length of the body (female) or long dark brown tails twice the body length (male); body with the rear two-thirds cream and the rest dark brown (female) or blackish-brown with lighter ribbing (male); clear wings; pale cream legs. Resembles *Caenis* and summer and fall *Paraleptophlebia* species (spinners).

Emergence

Tricos usually begin hatching in mid-July when spotted knapweed, mullein, wild onion, and wild rhododendron are blooming and continue emerging until the end of October, until the first or second frost. Male duns emerge the night before mating takes place, somewhere between 10 PM and 2 AM. Female duns emerge early in the morning—from 6 to 9 AM—depending on the air temperature. Mating, egg laying, and the spinnerfall usually occur between 7 and 10 AM, but this timing can be accelerated or delayed if the weather is unusually hot or cold. When anglers talk about fishing a Trico hatch, they are usually referring to the spinnerfall.

Behavior and Tactics

More fishing tactics have been developed around this hatch and spinnerfall than any other Pennsylvania mayfly species. But most anglers completely ignore Trico nymphs, even though a small weighted Pheasant Tail fished through riffles and pools in tandem with a larger more visible dry fly like an *Isonychia* parachute or Patriot can be effective. Trico nymphs can hatch just about anywhere in the stream: on the bottom, at the surface, or by crawling onto submerged rocks and vegetation.

Trout will feed on emerging female duns before the spinnerfall and you can catch them with #20–24 Comparaduns or thorax patterns fished on 6X or 7X tippets, but spinnerfalls provide the best fishing opportunities during the Trico hatch. Male spinners swarm about 10 to 20 feet above fast water. Females enter the swarm, mate, and then move out of the swarm (hovering 2 to 5 feet above the surface), flying upstream to lay their fertilized eggs. Mated females carry dark olive egg sacs. It's not always necessary to fish patterns tied specifically to imitate males or females, especially during the season's earliest Trico spinnerfalls. But after a few weeks, the trout often become more selective. You may have to fish a female spinner pattern (white or cream body) at the beginning of the spinnerfall and then switch to a male spinner pattern (black body) at the end to copy the males falling to the water.

Since Tricos hatch every day for several months with plenty of fishing pressure, trout get selective. Use a long 12- to 15-foot leader and 6X or finer tippet. Sometimes you may have to fish #26 rather than the standard #22 or #24. Small Trico patterns are difficult to see, so it helps to fish them in tandem with another, more visible, dry fly. You can also tie several Trico spinners to a larger hook (#16) to imitate a cluster of spinners. Other anglers set the hook whenever they see a rise near where they think their fly is. A slight lift of the rod tip is all that's needed. If you set too hard, and the fish hasn't taken your fly, you might scare it. But if the fish has taken the fly, and you set hard, you'll probably break it off.

Notes

Tricos are prolific on the state's limestone streams and are fairly common on many of the state's freestone streams. The heaviest Trico spinnerfalls occur in stream sections void of a heavy canopy, the presence of which would prevent the normal mating flight. Even a small opening in the tree cover along a shoreline can provide enough room for the Tricos to mate. Trico spinners and Summer Blue Quill spinners (pages 71–72) appear in the air 10 to 20 feet above the surface at the same time.

There are several species of Tricos (*Tricorythodes stygiatus, Tricorythodes minutus, Tricorythodes allectus, Tricorythodes fictus*), but from a fishing perspective, there is no need to be able to differentiate between them.

Premier Hatches

Letort Spring Run, Elk Creek (Lycoming County), Falling Springs Branch, Little Bushkill, Quittapahilla Creek, Tulpehocken Creek

Hebe

(aka Pale Evening Dun, Yellow Quill)
Leucrocuta hebe, prev. *Heptagenia hebe*
August 5–October 15 (afternoon/evening)
#16–18 (6–8 mm)

Biot Parachute

Hook: #16–80 standard dry fly
Thread: Yellow 8/0 Uni-Thread
Tail: Dun hackle fibers
Abdomen: PMP turkey biot
Post: White McFlylon or Antron
Thorax: PMP Super Fine
Hackle: Dun

Description

Nymphs: (Clinger) Pale gray tails (3), olive-brown body and legs with lighter markings, dark brown wing pads. **Dun:** Creamy yellow tails (2), bright yellow body and legs tinted with olive, and pale, light gray wings with dark gray venations. **Spinner:** Light gray tails (2), yellowish- to tannish-brown body, pale yellow legs, and clear wings with dark brown venations. Resembles *Leucrocuta Aphrodite* and *Ephemerella dorothea dorothea.*

Emergence

Hebes begin hatching in the summer when the goldenrod first blooms and last into the fall. Their initial emergences (usually during warm weather) often begin in the evening, or near dusk, after the air and water temperatures begin to cool. In the fall, Hebes often hatch in the afternoon because temperatures are cooler.

Behavior and Tactics

Nymphs prefer to live in slow- to moderate-flowing trout streams. Before the first hatches begin, dead-drift heavily weighted olive-brown Hare's Ear Nymphs on the bottom through braided water and where riffled water begins to slow into a pool. The nymphs' swimming ability is limited, and they migrate to slower water near shore, or in-stream obstructions, to emerge into duns just beneath the surface. Imitate the naturals by slowly stripping weighted flies toward the shore.

Once some duns begin to appear, fish an unweighted Pheasant Tail just below the surface to imitate nymphs emerging into duns. Dry-fly patterns tied with trailing shucks are generally less effective for imitating Hebe adults because the duns emerge subsurface. Spinnners usually fall at dusk during the summer and often provide the best dry-fly fishing opportunities for this hatch at this time of year. In cooler weather, common in the fall, spinners can fall in the afternoon.

Notes

Hebes are often misidentified as Sulphurs (*E. dorothea dorothea*) or Blue-Winged Olives because they are similar in size and color. Hebes only have two tails, and Sulphurs have three. Also, Hebe wings are pale with heavy, dark gray venations, but Sulphurs and BWOs have solid dun-colored wings without prominent venations.

Premier Hatches

Upper Delaware River, Bald Eagle Creek, Little Juniata River, Penns Creek

Big Slate Drake

Big Slate Drake dun

Hexagenia rigida spinner

(aka Hex)
Hexagenia atrocaudata
August 5–September 1 (after dark)
#6–10, 2XL (20–28 mm)

Gray Wulff

Hook:	#6–10, 2X-long dry fly
Thread:	Black 8/0 Uni-Thread
Tail:	Natural deer hair
Body:	Gray beaver dubbing
Wing:	Natural deer hair
Hackle:	Medium dun

Description

Nymph: (Burrower) Short tan tails (3), yellowish-tan belly with brown markings on back, dark brown wing pads, and tan legs with darker markings. **Dun:** Black tails (2) with a vestigial third tail, dark slate-gray body ribbed with yellow; dark gray wings with olive green reflections; dark brown front legs with yellow banding and tan rear legs. **Spinner:** Dark gray tails (2), tannish-gray body; pale gray wings; dark brown legs. Resembles *Isonychia bicolor* (though *Isonychia* are much smaller).

Emergence

Hexagenia atrocaudata is fairly common, particularly in larger rivers and streams, though it seldom appears in large numbers. Hatches begin in early August when goldenrod is just beginning to open, and continue throughout the month, overlapping with White Fly hatches. Duns emerge after dark. The spinners begin soaring high above the water and free-falling toward the surface like glider planes around 7 PM.

Behavior and Tactics

The large nymphs are sensitive to light and generally remain tucked in their burrows during the day, leaving only at dusk or at night (earlier in overcast weather) to feed or emerge. Well after dark, the nymphs swim to the surface with an exaggerated undulating movement to emerge into duns. Imitate the migrating nymphs with large, 2X-long heavily weighted tan Hare's Ears slowly stripped along the bottom. Since it will most likely be dark, forgo the indicator, and just try to feel the strike. This technique is most effective in the braided water below riffles, or in pools, where silt collects and the nymphs form their burrows. Another effective way to imitate the nymphs is with unweighted, or lightly weighted, Hare's Ears fished with short, quick strips to emulate the natural's undulating movements. Or slowly raise and lower your rod tip as the flies float through a pool to mimic the up-and-down motions of a nymph trying to free itself from its nymphal shuck. Use heavy tippet.

The huge spinners appear over the water in the evening, well before mating, laying eggs, and falling spent to the water. Trout don't start to feed on the spent spinners until after dark, but once they have been hatching for a week or more, trout will take large Hex spinner patterns fished at dusk, even though they won't feed on the real thing until later. After dark, huge Gray Wulffs dead-drifted or gently twitched in the vicinity of a trout work well. Antron-wing spinners work as well as anything to imitate the enormous spinners, but keep your tails short enough so that the stiff fibers don't prevent the fish from taking the fly.

Notes

Two Hex species are fairly common in Pennsylvania. The first is *H. atrocaudata*, which looks like a giant Slate Drake, and the second is *Hexagenia rigida*, which looks like a giant Yellow Drake. All *Hexagenia* species have three tails. Two are long and prominent, but the vestigial middle tail is short and hard to see.

Premier Hatches

Delaware River, French Creek, Little Lehigh, Loyalsock Creek, Penns Creek, Yellow Breeches Creek

White Fly

White Fly dun

Ephoron leukon
August 10–September 10 (evening)
#12–16 (9–12 mm)

Hi-Vis White Wulff

Hook: #12–16 standard dry fly
Thread: White 8/0 Uni-Thread
Tail: White calf tail
Body: Pale yellow or white beaver dubbing
Wing: Chartreuse calf tail
Hackle: Badger

Description

Nymph: (Burrower) Pale gray tails (3), body, and wing pads; cream legs. **Dun:** Three (male) or two (female) pale gray tales, pale cream, yellowish (female) or chalky white (male) body; pale gray wings; front pair of legs is dark brown and back two pair are white. **Spinner (male only):** Pale gray tail (3); chalky white body, except the last two segments, which are dark brown; glassy clear wings; rear two pair of legs are white and front pair is dark brown.

Females are larger (about a size 14), and they have two tails. They also have a yellowish cast to their abdomens from the two large egg sacks they carry, appearing chalky white after they have deposited their eggs. Females have strange-looking atrophied legs that prevent them from landing. Males have three tails and are slightly smaller than the females (about one hook size). The males' legs are also weak but functional enough to hold on to the females during mating. Resembles *Maccaffertium modestum,* and *M. pulchellum.*

Emergence

White Flies usually begin hatching round the second week of August when the goldenrod has been blooming for a week or more. The hatch continues for ten days to two weeks, lasting even longer on some waters. A few of the flies may start appearing over the water's surface around 7 or 8 PM. But the hatch builds as darkness approaches, and it continues well past dark on most evenings. Occasionally, there will be no visible White Flies until right at dark.

And then suddenly, in an explosion of life, the air fills with bugs and the trout begin to feed.

Behavior and Tactics

E. leukon nymphs are sensitive to light, and they seldom leave their burrows during the day. To prepare for their emergence, the nymphs leave their burrows about an hour before dark, and you can catch fish with heavily weighted, pale gray-colored Hare's Ears dead-drifted or slowly stripped along the stream bottom before the hatch begins. At dusk, the nymphs undulate toward the surface, pausing approximately 10 to 12 inches below it, and begin drifting as they attempt to free themselves from their nymphal shucks. Fish nymphs the same way as you would emerging Green Drake nymphs (see pages 52–55). Perhaps the most effective method for fishing near the beginning of an evening's White Fly hatch is with a tandem. Drop a lightly weighted Hare's Ear 6 to 10 inches below a White Wulff, and fish this rig at the tails of riffle and through the pools.

Once they emerge and escape from the water, the males transform into spinners and both sexes begin the search for an acceptable mate. All the mating activity takes place just a foot to a few feet above the surface, so it is easy to discern whether or not it's a White Fly hatch. The males fall spent to the water immediately after mating. The females lay their eggs, and then they too fall spent.

Intense White Fly hatches and spinnerfalls cause two major problems for anglers. First, there are often so many real flies on the water that it's difficult to get the trout to notice an artificial fly pattern. Second, because much of the best dry-fly action takes place well after dark, it's often difficult for anglers to see their fly patterns to know if they are casting into a trout's feeding lane or if a fish has eaten the fly.

Oversized Hi-Vis White Wulffs (#12) are easier for you to see after dark and stand out a little better for fish. Cut back your tippet to 4X to have the extra strength for landing the larger trout that feed after dark. Trout also rise to a White Wulff skittered across the surface during the hatch/spinnerfall. When a rising trout won't take your fly, try dragging the fly just a few inches above the rise to induce a take.

Regardless how many bugs you have seen that evening, if there are White Flies in the spider webs or collected in back eddies from the night before, do not leave until you are sure that the hatch won't be occurring. That means you must stay until dark. Look for rising fish in unusual places after dark. The trout's natural wariness during the day diminishes after the sun sets. Trout will feed in shallow water a few inches from the bank, or even within a rod's length of you.

Notes

Ephoron leukon prefers warmer sections of clean rivers and streams, mainly in central and south-central trout streams. It is especially abundant on the Susquehanna, Juniata, and Delaware Rivers. Look for the hatch to appear on the lower ends of many of the cooler tributaries to these rivers. Often fish have vacated the warmer sections of streams by the time the flies begin to emerge unless the weather has been cool.

Only male White Flies change from duns to spinners. A dead giveaway that you are experiencing a White Fly hatch is when you see males flying upstream, a few feet above the surface, still attached to their subimagal pellicle, which look like parachutes. Females are sexually mature adults after they transform into duns and do not molt into spinners.

Premier Hatches

Delaware River, Lehigh River, Little Juniata River, Neshannock Creek, Slippery Rock Creek, Yellow Breeches Creek

JAY NICHOLS PHOTO

5 Caddisflies

Caddisflies are divided into five families, which differ according to their larval habitats. Tube-case makers live in round or rectangular-shaped cases that they construct by gluing together minute bits of plant material or sand and small rocks. Net spinners build silken nets to collect food. Beside their nets, they construct small homes from bits of sand or pebbles, where they live between feedings. Free-living caddisflies, the simplest of all caddis families, do not build homes. They generally wander beneath rocks, just like many mayfly and stonefly species. Purse-case makers live as free-living caddisflies until their final instar. After their final instar, purse-case makers construct a rounded case from plant or rocky material where they live until they hatch into adults. Most of these caddisflies are small, and anglers often refer to them as "microcaddis." Finally, saddle-case makers construct semicircular cases, resembling a shell, out of larger pebbles.

The caddisfly's life cycle is complete. A mayfly changes directly from a nymph into a winged, subadult (called a subimago). The caddisfly's life cycle has an extra step. A caddisfly hatches from an egg and becomes a larva. The larva feeds and grows throughout the year, usually molting five times.

At approximately the same time each year, depending upon the species, the larva begins its transformation to adult on the stream bottom, inside a pupal shuck. This metamorphosis from larva to pupa (called a resting stage) lasts from several days to a few weeks, again depending upon the species. Once the pupa is fully formed, it

PENNSYLVANIA CADDISFLY HATCH CHART

Scientific Name	Common Name
Chimarra aterrima	Little Black Caddis
Brachycentrus fuliginosus and *B. numerosus*	Grannom
Brachycentrus appalachia	Apple Caddis
Psilotreta spp.*	Cream Caddis
Rhyacophila lobifera	Green Sedge, Green Caddis
*Deplectona modesta**	Dark Brown Caddis
Hydropsyche spp. and *Symphitopsyche slossonae*	Spotted Sedge, Tan Caddis
Cheumatopsyche spp.	Little Sister Sedge
Psilotreta labida and *P. frontalis*	Dark Blue Sedge
Pycnopsyche spp.	October Caddis

*Minor hatches, Emerges: M = morning, LM = late morning, A = afternoon,

chews through its shuck and crawls, drifts, or swims toward the surface, shedding the shuck in the process. The pupa eventually breaks the water's surface film as a fully formed, sexually mature adult. The adult flies to streamside vegetation, where it finishes drying and prepares to mate.

Male and female caddisflies gather over riffles to mate while they're flying. After mating, the males die, the females deposit their eggs, and then they also die. Some females drop their eggs on the water's surface by fluttering and dipping their egg sack until it falls free. Others swim or crawl to the stream bottom to distribute their eggs. This life cycle, from egg to mating and laying eggs, is usually completed in one year. But some species, like *Psilotreta labida*, have a two-year life cycle.

Hatch Date	Time of Day	Size
March 1–May 20	A	#16–18
Apr. 10–May 15	M, A	#12–16
Apr. 10–May 15	A	#14–16
May 1–June 20	M, A	#14
May 1–Aug. 30	A, E	#14–16
May 15–July 1	M, A	#12
May 15–Aug. 20	M, A	#14–18
May 15–June 15	M, A, E	#16–20
May 15–June 20	LA, E	#12–14
Sept. 20–Oct. 20	E, LE	#10

LA = late afternoon, E = evening, LE = late evening/night

JAY NICHOLS PHOTO

Grannoms are the first big hatch of the year on many trout streams.

Little Black Caddis

JAY NICHOLS PHOTO

Little Black Caddis

Chimarra aterrima
March 1–May 20 (afternoon)
#16–18 (6–8 mm)

CDC Scud Caddis

Hook:	#16–18 scud
Thread:	Black 8/0 Uni-Thread
Body:	Black beaver dubbing
Wing:	Medium dun CDC

Description

Larva: (Net Spinner) Amber to orange body. **Pupa/Adult:** Dark brown to black body; black to dark gray wings; dark brown to black legs. Resembles several *Brachycentrus* species and *Psilotreta labida*, but *P. labida* is much larger.

Emergence

Chimarra emerge from early March to late May when forsythia start to bloom, beginning each day around noon and continuing through the afternoon.

Behavior and Tactics

Chimarra spend most of their lives beneath rocks, feeding on small particles trapped in their nets. But they travel to the tops of their rocky homes and crawl, or swim, to shallow areas near shore to emerge. Dead-drift standard orange beadheads and Bird of Prey larva patterns along the river bottom or slowly strip them toward shore, before and during an emergence. Adults, when they first emerge, are generally less important to anglers because trout may not be holding in shallow areas near shore (where the adults emerge) at this time of year. But egg-laying females can provide fantastic dry-fly opportunities when they fall helplessly to the water after depositing their eggs, providing an easy meal for trout. These spent caddisflies are best imitated by dead-drifting CDC Scud Caddis patterns to sipping fish.

Notes

Chimarra caddis live throughout Pennsylvania, usually in medium to large creeks and rivers. Their hatches sometimes overlap with *Baetis,* Blue Quill, and Hendricksons. Their hatches are often overshadowed by Hendricksons, frustrating anglers casting mayfly patterns to trout selectively feeding on caddis.

Premier Hatches

Falling Springs Branch, French Creek, Laurel Hill Creek, Little Juniata River, Octoraro Creek, Monacacy Creek, Ninemile Run, Penns Creek, Ridley Creek, Upper Delaware River, Yellow Breeches Creek

Grannom

Brachycentrus numerosus and *B. fuliginosus*
April 10–May 15 (morning/afternoon)
#12–16 (7–13 mm)

Peacock Caddis

Hook:	#12–16 standard dry fly
Thread:	Black 8/0 Uni-Thread
Body:	Peacock herl
Wing:	Deer hair
Hackle:	Brown and grizzly

Description

Larva: (Tube-Case Maker) Brown head, bright green body. **Pupa/Adult:** Greenish-black body, mottled brown wings, greenish-black legs. Resembles *Chimarra atterima* and *Psilotreta labida.*

Emergence

Grannoms emerge in mid-April at the same time marsh marigolds and forsythia are in bloom. They hatch late morning to midday and continue through the afternoon. They can coincide with the end of the Hendricksons and the beginning of the March Browns.

Behavior and Tactics

Larvae live in well-oxygenated areas of current inside dark brown tubes created from bits of plant matter and shaped like flat-sided ice cream cones or oil derricks. The pupae swim to the surface film to emerge into adults. Trout sometimes ignore the newly hatched adults on the surface, opting to feed on the subsurface larva and pupa. Dead-drift green beadheads and Bird of Prey larva imitations or swing wet flies through riffles.

Egg-laying females provide an easy meal for trout when the river bottom isn't full of larva and pupa. The females fall helplessly to the river's surface as they try to rid themselves of their egg ball. Imitate this behavior by either dead-drifting or gently twitching Peacock, Elk Hair, and Henryville dry-fly caddis patterns.

Notes

Grannoms are closely related to the Apple Caddis, though they are darkly colored and much more widespread in Pennsylvania than the light-colored Apple Caddis. Hatches often overlap with Apple Caddis emergences in streams where both species are present.

Premier Hatches

Allegheny River, Big Bushkill Creek, Big Fishing Creek, Bowman Creek, Delaware River, Driftwood Branch of the Sinnemahoning, Dyberry Creek, Honey Creek, Kishacoquillas Creek, Little Juniata River, Little Pine Creek, Little Sandy Creek, Mud Run, Penns Creek, Pohopoco Creek, Slippery Rock Creek, Spruce Creek, Sugar Creek

Apple Caddis

Apple Caddis

(aka Shad Fly)
Brachycentrus appalachia
April 10–May 15 (afternoon)
#14–16 (11–13 mm)

Trude Wing Caddis

Hook: #14–16 standard dry fly
Thread: Black 8/0 Uni-Thread
Body: Apple green beaver dubbing
Wing: Bleached elk hair
Hackle: Medium dun

Description

Larva: (Tube-Case Maker) Brown head, bright green body. **Pupa/Adult:** Apple green abdomen, medium ginger thorax and legs, cream to light tan wings.

Emergence

Apple Caddis usually live in medium to large creeks and rivers. Their emergence, from late April to mid-May, begins late morning to midday and continues through the afternoon. They appear when apple trees are heavily budded and in bloom and Black Quills are hatching.

Behavior and Tactics

Larvae live in well-oxygenated areas of current, inside brown tubes created from bits of plant matter and shaped like flat-sided ice cream cones. Pupae swim to the surface film to emerge into adults. Dead-drift green beadhead larva and Bird of Prey larva imitations or swing wet flies through the riffles to imitate the larvae and pupae.

Trout sometimes ignore the thousands of newly hatched Apple Caddis adults on the surface, opting to feed subsurface on the larvae and pupae. Egg-laying Apple Caddis, near the end of their yearly emergence, provide an easy meal for trout when the river bottom isn't full of larvae and pupae. The females often fall helplessly to the river's surface as they try to rid themselves of their egg ball. Imitate this behavior by either dead-drifting or gently twitching Trude Wing, Elk Hair, and Spun Head Deer Hair caddis patterns.

Notes

The Apple Caddis gets its name from its bright green, apple-colored abdomen. Though uncommon throughout Pennsylvania, it can be important in the watersheds where it lives. The species is similar to Grannoms, differing only in their coloration. The two hatches often overlap, and sometimes coincide with the end of the Hendrickson and beginning of the March Brown mayflies.

In the Upper Delaware River system, Apple Caddis often emerge during the American shad migration to the trout sections of the river, earning them the local name "Shad Fly." The use of this colloquialism creates a good argument for the importance of using scientific nomenclature when discussing aquatic insect hatches. In much of central Pennsylvania, including the Penns Creek watershed, the term "Shad Fly" is used for the Green Drake dun (*Ephemera guttalata*).

Premier Hatches

Big Bushkill Creek, Delaware River

Green Sedge

JOHN MILLIER PHOTO

Rhyacophila lobifera (and related species)
May 1–August 30 (afternoon/evening)
#14–16 (8–18 mm)

Henryville Caddis

Hook: #14–16 standard dry fly
Thread: Tan 8/0 Uni-Thread
Body: Olive or green floss palmered with grizzly hackle
Wing: Gray mallard
Hackle: Brown

Description

Larva: (Free Living) Brown head, bright green body. **Pupa/Adult:** Medium olive to green body, light brown wings, medium olive to green legs.

Emergence

Green Sedges hatch in early May and continue until late August. Spring hatches usually begin in late morning or early afternoon and last until dark. Summer hatches often occur earlier in the morning and in the evening. Hatches usually begin when redbud starts to bloom, lilacs are getting ready to bloom, and the Big Sulphur appears.

Behavior and Tactics

Larvae live in riffles and other swift-flowing sections of water and roam beneath rocks, anchored to the river bottom by a light brown silk line. To imitate those that sometimes lose their hold and are swept into the fast currents, dead-drift bright green beadheads and Bird of Prey larva imitations through riffles. Pupae are strong swimmers and trout feed on them as they drift and swim toward the surface, preparing to emerge. Imitate them by swinging wet flies.

Henryville, X Caddis, and Elk Hair Caddis imitations fished with a dead drift in riffles, or skittered, will accurately imitate the adults, which hatch in great numbers. Females dive or crawl to the stream bottom to lay their eggs, and then slowly drift spent to the surface. Imitate these submerged adults by adding split-shot or beads to standard dry flies fished dead-drift.

Notes

Hatches, due to their lengthy duration, can overlap with many mayfly and caddis species. But they are most important to fishermen when they hatch in streams with limited aquatic insect life. The Green Sedge is fairly common in all regions of Pennsylvania, though it is found intermittently from stream to stream.

Premier Hatches

Mud Run, Octoraro Creek, Slippery Rock Creek, Spring Creek, Tulpehocken Creek, Upper Delaware River

Spotted Sedge

Spotted Sedge

(aka Tan Caddis)
Hydropsyche spp. and *Symphitopsyche slossonae*
May 15–August 20 (morning/afternoon)
#14–18 (8–15 mm)

X Caddis

Hook:	#14–18 standard dry fly
Thread:	Tan 8/0 Uni-Thread
Tail:	Ginger Antron
Body:	Tan beaver dubbing
Wing:	Deer hair

Description

Larva: (Net Spinner) Brown head and back, olive belly. **Pupa/Adult:** Creamish-tan to light brown body and legs and light brown wings. Resembles *Cheumatopsyche* (but *Hydropsyche* and *Symphitopsyche slossonae* are larger, and more bland in color).

Emergence

These species are some of the most important and prolific in Pennsylvania. Collectively, they form a long-lasting group of insects, which begin hatching in mid- to late spring when dame's rocket is just starting to bloom and continue throughout the summer and into the early fall. Early hatches often occur with the March Brown, though because of the long emergence period of the many species, hatches will overlap many other aquatic insects.

Behavior and Tactics

Larvae prefer to live in riffles and runs, anchored to submerged rocks with a silk line. They are difficult to imitate with artificial flies because of the way in which they dangle in the current. Gary LaFontaine expressed several ideas in his book *Caddisflies* to imitate this behavior, including coloring tippets white to suggest the anchoring line. But dead-drifted olive beadheads and Bird of Prey larva imitations work well to imitate the naturals drifting with the current before swimming toward the surface to molt into adults. Adults often remain on the water's surface for extended periods as they try to recover from molting. Adult females dive to the river bottom to lay their eggs and then float to the surface, drifting spent like a spinner in the film. Dry-fly patterns work well when the caddis first molt into adults and when they return to lay eggs. Dead-drift X Caddis and CDC Caddis to imitate the adults and spent egg-layers. Swing wet-fly patterns to imitate the diving egg-layers, or dead-drift weighted dry-fly patterns to imitate adults that have finished laying their eggs.

Notes

These species are more tolerant of certain types of pollutants, such as sewage effluent and farming run-off, than most aquatic insect species, which allows them to thrive in many Pennsylvania trout streams where other aquatic species cannot.

Weather can dictate the timing of this hatch (and most other caddis hatches as well). If the air and water temperatures are unusually warm, the hatch may not begin until early evening, or it may wait till morning. During cloudy, cool weather the hatch will sometimes occur in the afternoon.

Premier Hatches

Bowman Creek, Brodhead Creek, Cedar Run, Clearfield Creek, Delaware River, Fishing Creek, Hoagland Branch, Honey Creek, Kishacoquillas Creek, Lycoming Creek, Oil Creek, Penns Creek, Slippery Rock Creek, Spring Creek, Young Woman's Creek

Little Sister Sedge

Little Sister Sedge

(aka Olive Caddis)
Cheumatopsyche spp.
May 15–June 15 (morning/afternoon/evening)
#16–20 (7–12 mm)

CDC Caddis

Hook: #16–20 standard dry fly
Thread: Olive 8/0 Uni-Thread
Body: Olive beaver dubbing
Wing: Medium dun CDC
Over Wing: White CDC
Hackle/Legs: Medium dun CDC

Description

Larva: (Net Spinner) Brown head, olive body. **Pupa/Adult:** Olive brown body and legs and light brown wings. Resembles *Hydropsyche* and *Symphitopsyche slossonae.*

Emergence

This important group of insects usually hatches from mid-May to mid-June, when lilacs are in bloom. But they are often overlooked by anglers who are concentrating on the famous mayflies that also hatch during this period, such as March Browns. *Cheumatopsyche* spp. are similar to *Hydropsyche* spp. and *Symphitopsyche slossonae,* but can live in warmer and even more nutrient-rich sections of streams and rivers. Hatches can occur in the morning or evening.

Behavior and Tactics

This species received its common name "Little Sister Sedge" because it closely resembles the physical nature and hatching characteristics of the *Hydropsyche* and *Symphitopsyche slossanae* species. The same fishing techniques for *Hydropsyche* and *Symphitopsyche slossanae* species apply for *Cheumatopsyche* spp. The only significant differences between these two types of caddisflies are their size, body color, and that *Cheumatopsyche* hatches usually end by mid-June.

Notes

The small size combined with its overlapping emergence with many famous mayfly species make this caddis easy to miss.

Premier Hatches

Spring Creek, Penns Creek, Shenango River, Tulpehocken Creek, Upper Delaware River, Youghiogheny River

Dark Blue Sedge

Dark Blue Sedge

Psilotreta labida and *P. frontalis*
May 15–June 20 (late afternoon/evening)
#12–14 (12–15 mm)

Spun Head Deer Hair Caddis

Hook: #12–14 standard dry fly
Thread: Black 8/0 Uni-Thread
Body: Black beaver dubbing
Wing: Dark dun deer hair
Head: Spun and clipped dark dun deer hair

Description

Larva: (Tube-Case Makers) Gray head, green body. **Pupa/Adult:** Dark bluish-gray body with green reflections; dark bluish-gray wings; dark gray legs with green reflections. Resembles *Chimarra* spp., but *Psilotreta labida* is much larger and tinted with green reflections.

Emergence

Psilotreta labida usually emerges in late afternoon and evening from mid-May to mid-June when oxeye daisies are just starting to bloom. This hatch coincides with Green Drake and Sulphur hatches, and often appears with the Slate Drake.

Behavior and Tactics

Larvae have a two-year life cycle and live in small tube-shaped structures, which they construct from bits of sand and gravel. Dozens of them migrate to shared rocks before they either crawl or swim to the surface to emerge. Look for rocks in the streambed that contain masses of *Psilotreta* cases to determine the best locations to fish the hatch. The pupae often wiggle and twitch on, or just below, the surface, and trout find this movement irresistible. Imitate this behavior by twitching dry caddis patterns about 1 foot in front of rising fish, though it's more effective to dangle wet and dry flies downstream in the current to imitate this behavior. Allow the flies to swing below you, but do not strip them back immediately. The current will hold them near the surface as the line tightens, and the flies will undulate just beneath, and in, the surface film. Skitter an Elk Hair Caddis across the water's surface to imitate the adult females dipping and fluttering on the surface when they return to lay their eggs.

Notes

Their dark coloration (sometimes camouflaging them on the water) combined with simultaneous emergences of mayflies make hatches difficult to detect. Anglers often misdiagnose trout rising to the caddis and cast mayfly patterns to unsympathetic, rising fish.

Premier Hatches

Bowman Creek, Clarion River, Cove Creek, Dyberry Creek, First Fork of the Sinnemahoning, Kishacoquillas Creek, Little Juniata River, Lower Bald Eagle, Muncy Creek, Neshannock Creek, Penns Creek, Tunkhannock Creek, Upper Delaware River

October Caddis

October Caddis

(aka Great Brown Autumn Sedge)
Pycnopsyche spp., prev. *Stenophylax* spp.
September 20–October 20 (evening or night)
#10 (19–22 mm)

CDC Palmered Elk Hair Caddis

Hook: #10 Daiichi standard dry fly
Thread: Orange 8/0 Uni-Thread
Body: Tannish orange beaver dubbing
Hackle: Ginger CDC
Wing: Orange deer hair

Description

Larva: (Tube-Case Makers) Brown head, ginger body. **Pupa/Adult:** Tannish-orange body and wings, pale yellowish-orange legs. Resembles *Hydropsyche* and *Symphitopsyche* but are much larger and a deeper orange color.

Emergence

Adults hatch in late September after the goldenrod has been open for couple of weeks. October Caddis hatches will sometimes overlap with sporadic mayfly emergences of *Isonychia bicolor, Acentrella turbida,* and *Leucrocuta hebe.* Though October Caddis emerge at night, they can also hatch (in smaller numbers) in the evening and morning.

Behavior and Tactics

Larvae eat decomposing leaves from trees and construct large cases from pieces of sticks and other plant debris. They live in slow-moving, placid stream sections where leafy material collects on the stream bottom. Swinging October Caddis Bird of Prey larvae patterns through riffles in the morning or evening will sometimes catch fish, so it's worth trying if the fishing has been slow with other techniques. However, it's generally more effective to blind-cast large, orange Elk Hair Caddis in riffles—dead-drifting, twitching, and skittering the flies. It takes a bit of faith to fish October Caddis patterns, because few (or maybe no) naturals will be visible during the day.

Notes

October Caddis live in cold streams and rivers, usually in forested areas. They provide a good-size meal when few other aquatic insects are readily available, making them important for fishermen, though the insects seldom hatch in large numbers.

Premier Hatches

Big Fishing Creek, Penns Creek, Spruce Creek, Upper Delaware River

Stoneflies, such as these Golden Stoneflies, mate on the ground, not in flight like mayflies and caddisflies.

PAUL WEAMER PHOTO

6 Stoneflies

Stonefly nymphs hatch from an egg and spend one to three years maturing, depending upon species, before emerging, mating, and laying eggs. They have an incomplete lifecyle (like mayflies) and don't pupate. Stonefly nymphs freely wander beneath rocks in search of food. At approximately the same time each year (date depends upon species), stonefly nymphs crawl to exposed rocks or vegetation to molt into adults. Some species will also emerge subsurface if conditions prevent them from reaching dry areas. The adults then fly or crawl to streamside vegetation to prepare to mate.

Stoneflies mate on the ground, not in flight like mayflies and caddisflies. They are generally poor flyers, and that may contribute to their land-bound mating practices. Males die quickly after mating, and egg-bearing females often lay their eggs near stream banks. Stonefly species that deposit their eggs in riffles begin the process during periods of low light, early in the morning or at night. Mating stoneflies do not fall spent to the water like mayflies and caddisflies, so they do not offer the trout an opportunity to eat them once the act is completed.

PENNSYLVANIA STONEFLY HATCH CHART

Scientific Name	Common Name
Allocapnia and *Capnia vernalis**	Little Black Stonefly
Taeniopteryx nivalis	Little Black Stonefly
Strophopteryx fasciata	Little Brown Stonefly
Isoperla and *Acroneuria* spp. and *Paragnetina immarginata*	Golden Stonefly
Pteronarcys dorsata	Giant Stonefly
Alloperla imbecilla	Lime Sally
Isoperla bilineata	Yellow Sally

*Minor hatches, Emerges: M = morning, LM = late morning, A = afternoon,

Small stonefly patterns

Rubber Leg Copper John and Kyle's Yellow Sally Nymph. For recipes, see Appendix, page 148.

Hatch Date	Time of Day	Size
Feb. 15–March 31	M, A	#16–20
Feb. 20–Apr. 15	A	#12–18
March 15–Apr. 25	A	#14–16
May 5–June 30	E	#8–12
May 20–June 15	E	#4–8
June 1–Aug. 10	A	#14–16
June 1–Aug. 10	A	#14–16

LA = late afternoon, E = evening, LE = late evening/night

Large stonefly patterns

Jumbo John and Rubber Leg Beadhead Stonefly Nymph. For recipes, see Appendix, page 149.

Little Black Stonefly

Little Black Stonefly

(aka Early Black Stonefly)
Taeniopteryx nivalis
February 20–April 15 (afternoon)
#12–18 (9–14 mm)

Elk Hair Caddis

Hook: #12–18 standard dry fly
Thread: Black 8/0 Uni-Thread
Body: Black beaver dubbing
Hackle: Black
Rib (optional): Oval silver wire (fine)
Wing: Elk hair

Description

Nymph: Black tails, body, and legs; wing cases are black mottled with brown. **Adult:** Black tails, body, and legs; light dun wings with black venations. Resembles *Allocapnia* spp., *Capnia* spp., and *Strophopteryx fasciata.*

Emergence

Little Black Stoneflies usually begin their late February emergence near the end of the much less angler-important *Allocapnia* and *Capnia* stoneflies. *Capnia* stoneflies have partially formed wings, so they can't fly. They're smaller—size 18 to 20—and often crawl on top of snow and ice near a stream, not the water's surface. *Capnia* nymphs migrate to the frozen edges of a stream to emerge, outside the range of most trout that are usually holding in deeper water at this time.

Taeniopteryx nivalis usually emerges in cold rivers and streams from late morning through midafternoon, and hatches are best on warm, sunny days. Snowdrops, one of the first flowers of spring, and trailing arbutus are in bloom.

Behavior and Tactics

Trout often eat adults on the water's surface because some of them hatch in-river, despite the common belief that all stonefly species crawl to riverside rocks to emerge. Although adults are available on the surface of many Pennsylvania trout streams, anglers will usually fare better using nymphs because the cold water reduces the trout's metabolism, making them less inclined to chase their meals on the surface. Dead-drift Copper Johns and Pheasant Tails slow and deep to interest sluggish fish.

Stonefly adults buzz and skitter across the surface, behavior imitated by skittering a small, black Elk Hair Caddis across the surface. A late winter or early spring day with warm sunshine and a steady breeze is a great time to find trout rising to the adults. When the sun warms the water, the insects and the trout become more active, and the breeze blows more adults onto the water. In cold water, trout are more sluggish and a Flat-Water Stonefly is a better option for rising fish.

Notes

Taeniopteryx nivalis is one of the most common stonefly species in Pennsylvania and seems to be more pollution-tolerant than most other stoneflies. Many streams with reduced water quality from coal mining and agricultural run-off have fishable hatches.

Premier Hatches

Bald Eagle Creek, Big Fishing Creek, Cedar Run, Clearfield Creek, Penns Creek, Ridley Creek, Laurel Hill Creek, Little Juniata River, Little Lehigh, Spring Creek, Upper Delaware River

Little Brown Stonefly

Little Brown Stonefly

(aka Early Brown Stonefly)
Strophopteryx fasciata
March 15–April 25 (afternoon)
#14–16 (9–11 mm)

Flat-Water Stonefly

Hook: #14–16 standard dry fly
Thread: Brown 8/0 Uni-Thread
Body: Brown beaver dubbing
Rib (optional): Oval silver wire (fine)
Wing: Elk hair
Hackle: Brown

Description

Nymph: Brown tails, body, and legs; black wing cases mottled with brown. **Adult:** Brown tails, body, and legs; light dun wings with brown venations. Resembles *Taeniopteryx nivalis*.

Emergence

The Little Brown Stonefly hatches from mid-March to late April, often overlapping with the end of the *Taeniopteryx nivalis* hatch in rivers and creeks where both insects are present. At this time, the forsythia is heavily budded and the white-flowerd rue-anemone is fully open. Just like *Taeniopteryx nivalis, Strophopteryx fasciata* emerges from late morning through midafternoon (the warmest part of the day). A warm sunny day creates good hatching conditions for this insect, and usually increases the hatch's intensity and duration.

Behavior and Tactics

Nymphs crawl onto exposed rocks, snow, or ice to emerge. They are less likely to emerge in-river than *Taeniopteryx navalis,* but they will occasionally when high water prevents them from finding dry areas. Dead-drift Copper Johns or brown Hare's Ear Nymphs along the bottom or slowly retrieve them toward the shore. Although adults can drift on the surface (just like *Taeniopteryx nivalis*), you'll probably catch more fish if you use nymphs.

When fish are rising to adults on the surface, skitter a small brown Elk Hair Caddis or dead-drift a Flat-Water Stonefly to catch them. A late winter or early spring day with warm sunshine and a steady breeze increases your chances of finding trout rising to the adults.

Notes

Strophopteryx fasciata live throughout Pennsylvania and seems to require cleaner water than *Taeniopteryx nivalis,* so just because one of these stoneflies is present in a stream, doesn't mean that both will be found.

Premier Hatches

Allegheny River, Bowman Creek, Caldwell Creek, Clark Creek, Clearfield Creek, Cove Creek, Cross Fork Creek, Driftwood Branch of the Sinnemahoning, Genesee Forks, Kettle Creek, Lackawaxen River, Lehigh River, Little Pine Creek, Loyalsock Creek, Lycoming Creek, Octoraro Creek, Pine Creek, Sixmile Run, Slate Run, Stony Fork Creek, Sugar Creek, Upper Delaware River

Golden Stonefly

Golden Stonefly

Female Golden Stonefly with eggs

(aka Light Stonefly, Brown Stonefly, Yellow Stonefly)
Isoperla and *Acroneuria* spp. and *Paragnetina immarginata*
May 5–June 30 (evening)
#8–12 (14–27 mm)

Swisher's Madam X

Hook: #8–12, 2X-long dry fly
Thread: Yellow 8/0 Uni-Thread
Tail: Deer hair
Body: Yellow floss or beaver dubbing
Wing: Deer hair
Legs: White or yellow round rubber

Description

Nymph: Yellow to golden brown tails; yellow body with olive and brown reflections; brown wing case mottled with yellow; yellow to golden brown legs. **Adult:** Yellow tails, body, and legs (*I. signata* has brownish-yellow body and legs); light dun wings with brown venations. Resembles *Pteronarcys dorsata.* Anglers sometimes confuse Golden Stoneflies with Giant Stoneflies because both insects can be large and vary in color.

Emergence

Golden Stonefly species comprise a large group of insects with a long hatching duration, lasting from late spring into July. Adults first appear at dusk or during the night in mid-May and coincide with the Green Drake hatch, shortly after dame's rocket begins blooming.

Behavior and Tactics

Most Golden Stoneflies have a two- to three-year life cycle, depending on the species. They crawl to streamside rocks (and even concrete bridge piers) and vegetation to emerge, generally during low light at, or after, sunset, though they will sometimes emerge during the day if it's cloudy. Dead-drift Rubber Leg Beadhead Stonefly Nymphs during high to moderate stream flows in the winter and early spring or slowly strip them toward the stream banks during an emergence. Adults are clumsy fliers and often fall onto the water's surface, creating opportunities to blind-cast large dry flies. Golden Stones provide a substantial meal to trout, and fish continue to take imitations (Madam Xs or Stimulators) throughout the summer and fall, well after the hatch has ended for the season. For this reason, a Golden Stonefly pattern with a nymph dropper is a great choice for blind-casting during the summer.

Notes

Golden Stoneflies hatch throughout Pennsylvania, but they generally live in swift-flowing riffles and runs of clean, cold streams adjacent to forests.

Premier Hatches

Big Fishing Creek, Bowman Creek, Cedar Run, Kettle Creek, Loyalsock Creek, Penns Creek, Slate Run, Upper Delaware River, Young Woman's Creek

Giant Stonefly

Giant Stonefly

(aka Eastern Salmon Fly)
Pteronarcys dorsata
May 20–June 15 (evening)
#4–8 (23–40 mm)

Sofa Pillow

Hook: #4–8, 2X-long dry fly
Thread: Orange 8/0 Uni-Thread
Tail: Elk hair
Body: Orange floss or beaver dubbing
Palmered Hackle: Brown
Rib (optional): Oval copper wire (fine)
Wing: Elk hair
Hackle: Brown (oversized)

Description

Nymph: Black tails, body, and legs; wing cases are black mottled with brown. **Adult:** Black tails and legs; orange body mottled with black; light dun wings with black venations. Resembles Golden Stonefly.

Emergence

Giant Stoneflies emerge near the end of May when oxeye daisies and blue violets are blooming and spring Isos are hatching, though you may see a few as early as late April. They are sensitive to light and often appear near dusk or at night, but they can also emerge during the day during overcast weather.

Behavior and Tactics

Dead-drift black Rubber Leg Beadhead Stonefly Nymphs throughout the year, whenever the water is high or off-color and in larger rivers with deep riffles. Though the emerging nymphs are large, Giant Stoneflies have a three-year life cycle, so nymphs are available to trout in various sizes throughout the year. Slowly strip nymph patterns toward the banks during the hatch's peak to imitate nymphs that are moving toward riverside rocks to emerge.

Giant Stonefly adults aren't always available to trout because they often emerge on exposed rocks, but they will emerge in-stream if necessary. Giant Stoneflies are clumsy fliers. And fishing during windy days, or in river sections with overhanging vegetation, will increase your chances of finding trout eating Giant Stonefly adults that are blown, or fall, into the river. Blind-casting large Sofa Pillows or Stimulators can be effective at this time. Mating takes place on dry ground, usually on rocks or in streamside vegetation, and females often lay their eggs by dipping their abdomens into the water from shore, so mating flights are generally unimportant for anglers.

Notes

The largest stonefly species in North America, *Pteronarcys dorsata* seldom emerges in large numbers and is therefore often overlooked by anglers. Because of their great size, many anglers associate them with only large rivers and creeks, but some small streams also have fishable hatches.

Premier Hatches

Bowman Creek, East Fork of the Sinnemahoning, Penns Creek, Slippery Rock Creek, Smays Run, Stonycreek River, Upper Delaware River, Wills Creek, Young Woman's Creek

Yellow and Lime Sallies

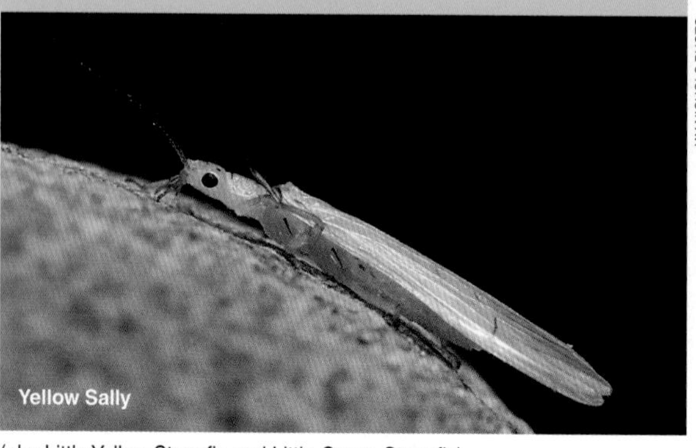
JAY NICHOLS PHOTO

Yellow Sally

(aka Little Yellow Stonefly and Little Green Stonefly)
Isoperla bilineata and *Alloperla imbecilla*
June 1–August 10 (afternoon)
#14–16 (8–10 mm)

Stimulator

Hook: #14–16, 2X-long dry fly
Thread: Orange, yellow, or green 8/0 Uni-Thread
Tail: Elk hair
Abdomen: Bright yellow beaver dubbing or floss
Abdomen Hackle: Brown
Rib: Copper wire
Wing: Elk hair
Thorax: Bright orange yarn, beaver dubbing, or floss
Thorax Hackle: Grizzly

Description

Nymph: Yellow or olive tails and legs, dirty yellow or olive body, and yellow or olive wing cases mottled with brown. **Adult:** Bright yellow or lime tails, body, and legs; pale yellow or pale green wings. Yellow and Lime Sallies appear almost identical to each other except for their color and live in the same habitat.

Emergence

These two brightly colored stonefly species live in cold, clean, swift-flowing creeks and rivers throughout the state. They both usually hatch from early June to mid-August when elderberry and chicory are opening and *Ephemera varia* is hatching. Though these insects prefer to hatch in low light, sporadic daytime emergences are common because the streams in which they live are generally shaded by dense forest canopy.

Behavior and Tactics

Yellow and Lime Sallies have a one-year life cycle. Their nymphs usually migrate toward shore and crawl to dry, in-stream rocks to emerge. Yellow and Lime Sallies seldom appear in large numbers, and they are often ignored by trout in waters with abundant aquatic insect populations. The best approach for fishing this hatch is to blind-cast sparsely tied Stimulators or Elk Hair Caddis in mountain brook and brown trout streams. These streams are generally less fertile, so the stoneflies are an important food source for trout. Green or yellow Kyle's Yellow Sally Nymphs can also be effective. Drop them off of the bend of a dry fly on short tippet to fish the nymphs in shallow water without hanging up.

Notes

Lime Sallies are generally less common and less prolific than Yellow Sallies.

Premier Hatches

Balls Creek, Bowman Creek, Cedar Run, Clark Creek, Cross Fork Creek, Elk Creek (for steelhead), Fishing Creek (Columbia County), Hayes Creek, Hickory Run, Hoagland Branch, Kettle Creek, Mehoopany Creek, Mud Run, Muncy Creek, Shehawken Creek, Slate Run, West Branch of the Clarion River, Young Woman's Creek

Midges are an extremely important year-round food source on many trout streams, especially the state's spring creeks.

JAY NICHOLS PHOTO

7 Craneflies and Midges

Though at first glance they may seem like night and day, craneflies (family Tipulidae) and midges belong to the same order of insects—Diptera, or two-winged flies. On average, cranefly larvae and adults are giants compared to the diminutive midges, though some craneflies are small and some midges are large. The subsurface life stages of both of these insects are vastly more important to trout and anglers than their adult stages. However, adult midges and adult craneflies can provide some great dry-fly fishing. Granted, adult midges provide much more action than adult cranes, but for some they are not nearly as much fun to fish. Adult craneflies, which resemble large mosquitoes, flit around in-stream rocks and bounce in undercuts after they have hatched. If you see splashy, aggressive rises, then fish are probably either feeding on caddis, stoneflies, or craneflies. No matter which particular insect they are feeding on, their rise form tells you that they are chasing their food, so a well presented, skittered, or skated hackle pattern would be a good choice for all three.

Midge adults are more important, especially on the state's spring creeks, where they can provide good dry-fly fishing throughout the year. Like with choosing a cranefly pattern, let the fish's rises tell you what to do. If you see small sipping rises and the water's surface seems void of mayflies or other easily seen bugs, look closer and you might discover that a small midge dry is a perfect choice. Because the subsurface stages of this insect are so important, we do include the Zebra Midge, which is one of Charlie's favorite patterns to fish in a tandem rig.

Craneflies

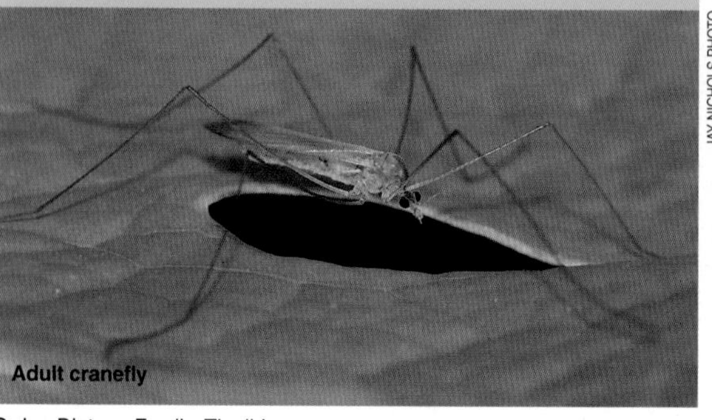
JAY NICHOLS PHOTO

Adult cranefly

Order: Diptera; Family: Tipulidae
#6–20 (5–50 mm)

Antolosky's Cranefly

(tied by Mark Antolosky)

Hook:	#12–20 short-shank dry fly
Thread:	Tan 8/0 Uni-Thread
Abdomen:	Cream Glo Bug Yarn
Thorax:	Fly Rite Sulphur dubbing
Hackle:	Brown
Wing:	Badger hackle tips

Description

Larva: Small, cigar-shaped worms in various shades of tan and olive. **Adult:** Six long legs, and two small wings that they generally keep folded over their backs. They are poor flyers and are often easy prey for birds and animals, including trout. Pennsylvania cranefly adults are 5 to 50 millimeters long, and can live up to fifteen days after hatching from larvae. The most prominent body colors for the adults are yellow, olive, and orange. Resembles midges and mosquitoes, though they do not bite.

Emergence

Craneflies may emerge anytime during the day from April to November, but they usually hatch in the afternoon during colder weather. As the weather and water warms, expect to find them in the morning and evening. Best hatches appear when dame's rocket first blooms and often coincide with Big Sulphur hatches.

Behavior and Tactics

In rising or high water, dead-drift Day's Cranefly Larva or Walt's Worms to imitate dislodged larvae. Adults are most important in streams with less diversity of aquatic insect life, like Spring Creek (Centre County). Adults are poor flyers and often fall onto the surface of the water. Exact imitations are a fly-tying challenge, but fortunately are not always necessary—any skittered fly such as a Stimulator or Variant work well. In healthy rivers like the Upper Delaware, where aquatic insect life is diverse and abundant, trout often ignore adult craneflies.

Notes

Craneflies, a vast group of mosquitolike insects that live in most Pennsylvania trout streams, are the largest family of true flies. Approximately 300 of the 1,500 known North American cranefly species have been identified in Pennsylvania. Of these, 107 are known to live in aquatic habitats as larva, making them potentially important to fly fishermen. They are most often found in clean rivers and streams lined with trees. Many species also live on or near streambanks and may be washed into the water during high flows associated with runoff and heavy rains. Egg-laying craneflies can appear in massive numbers at dusk. Many anglers miss these insects on the water, believing that the trout are feeding on spent mayfly spinners.

Premier Hatches

Big Fishing Creek, Penns Creek, Spring Creek, Upper Delaware River

Midges

JAY NICHOLS PHOTO

Adult midge

Order: Diptera; Family: Chironomidae
Year-round
#16–32 (2–15 mm)

Hi-Vis Midge

Hook:	#16–22 fine wire scud
Thread:	Olive 8/0 Uni-Thread
Rib:	Fine copper wire
Abdomen:	Olive 8/0 Uni-Thread
Wing:	Fluorescent pink Antron
Thorax:	Olive beaver dubbing
Hackle:	Grizzly

Zebra Midge

Hook:	#16–22, 2X-heavy scud
Bead:	Gold, copper, or silver
Thread:	Black 8/0 Uni-Thread
Abdomen:	Black thread
Rib:	Gold, copper, or silver wire
Thorax:	Black beaver dubbing

Description

Larva: Wormlike bodies are slightly tapered toward tails, not cigar-shaped like craneflies. Available in a wide range of colors, with black, olive, cream, yellow, gray, and red the most common. **Pupa/Adult:** Pupae are shorter, chunkier versions of the larvae with prominent thoraxes that house the adult's folded wings. Adults have six long legs, and two small light-colored wings that they generally keep folded over their backs. Male midge adults often have prominent, bushy antennae. Resembles craneflies and mosquitoes.

Emergence

Midges hatch all year, though warm afternoons when the weather is typically cold can be an excellent time to find fish rising to these diminutive insects.

Behavior and Tactics

Some larvae live in small cocoons, others are free-swimming, and some live on the stream bottom just like mayfly nymphs. Pupae live in the same habitats as the larvae. To match dislodged larvae or emerging pupae, dead-drift a Zebra Midge under an indicator or as a dropper on the bend of a dry fly. To imitate pupae emerging just under the surface, dead-drift small emerger patterns that hang just under the film. Sight-fish to rising trout with a single adult midge or a larger dry fly that imitates a cluster of adults, which is easier for you to see and provides the illusion of a larger mouthful for trout.

Notes

Midges live in nearly every type of water, from lakes and ponds, to rivers and creeks, and even outflows from sewage treatment plants. Though small, midges provide a dependable year-round food source for trout in many streams. Collect stream specimens to determine which colors are most prominent. Like mayflies, early and late season midges tend to be darker than summer midges.

Premier Hatches

Little Juniata River, Spring Creek, Yellow Breeches, Youghiogheny River

Grasshoppers and other terrestrials provide summertime sustenance for trout.

8 Terrestrials

The term "terrestrial" is used to encompass all land-dwelling insect species. These insects do not hatch in trout streams, so emerger fly patterns are unnecessary. Because terrestrials do not live in water, they must either fly, fall, hop, or be blown into the water for fish to have the opportunity to eat them. Terrestrials are important in all of Pennsylvania's trout streams, but they are particularly vital to trout living in streams with fewer aquatic insects.

The most prominent color of each terrestrial species listed in this section can vary greatly from region to region and stream to stream. Match specimens in your area.

Ants and Flying Ants

Carpenter ant

Order: Hymenoptera; Family: Formicidae
#12–24 (2–12 mm)

Parachute Ant

Hook: #12–24 standard dry fly
Thread: Black 8/0 Uni-Thread
Body: Black beaver dubbing
Wing: White Antron
Hackle: Grizzly or black

Bi-Color Epoxy Ant

Hook: #12–18, 2X-heavy wet fly
Thread: 8/0 Uni-Thread to match natural
Body: 6/0 Uni-Thread coated with epoxy
Hackle: Black or brown

Description

Ants can have black, red, or cinnamon bodies, or any combination of these colors. Wings on flying ants are clear or light dun colored. Flying ants resemble termites, but have three distinct body parts of the wingless ant, whereas termites have only two.

Emergence

Land-bound ants are available to trout from late spring, through the summer, until the first or second hard frost. Flying ants can usually be found on Pennsylvania trout streams within three days of August 25. They can appear any time after their initial flight, but they seem to prefer dry, hot, breezy weather. Flying ants appear just as the goldenrod is blooming and at the same time as the White Fly.

Behavior and Tactics

Ant colonies are made up of queens, workers, and male and female winged ants that have the sole purpose of reproducing to populate other colonies. Worker ants are sterile female ants who engage in the day-to-day activities (just about all of the activities) of tending to the queen, building and maintaining the nest, gathering the food, and protecting the colony. The females going about their work are the ants that we see most of the time.

At certain times of the year, the queen produces male and female ants that have wings. Male ants, also called drones, do nothing but eat and mate. When it is time to mate, the winged males and females will pour out of the ground or through the cracks in your sidewalk and take to the air. As the ants take to the sky, they meet and mate in swarms. After mating, the male ants shortly die. Where these ants swarm over water, the dying ants falling to water's surface can bring up all the trout in a given stretch. The females then land, drop their wings, and start new colonies.

Fish ants near overhanging vegetation where ants can fall or get swept into the water by the wind. Ants, both flying and nonflying, should be fished with a dead drift, near the shore, when prospecting for trout. Bi-Color Epoxy Ants, which are designed to sink, imitate insects that have fallen into the water and drowned in riffles, and should be fished with a dead drift like nymphs.

Premier Hatches

Most Pennsylvania trout streams

Grasshoppers

Grasshopper

Order: Orthoptera; Family: various families
#6–14, 2XL (15–40 mm)

Para-Hopper

Hook: #6–14, 2X-long dry fly
Thread: Tan 8/0 Uni-Thread
Abdomen: Yellow, tan, olive, or green dubbing
Over Wing: Mottled turkey wing quills
Legs: Knotted pheasant tail fibers
Post: White calf body
Hackle: Grizzly
Thorax: Yellow, tan, olive, or green dubbing

Description

Grasshoppers come in a wide range of colors (green, yellow, tan, and gray most common) and sizes and have long, thick bodies, two antennae, and powerful, prominent rear legs. Resembles katydids, which are large and bright green.

Emergence

Grasshoppers are available to trout from late spring and throughout the summer, until the first or second hard frost. They are found all over Pennsylvania, but are particularly plentiful along streams adjacent to fields or grassy areas within forests. Hoppers appear as long as milkweed is blooming and as soon as you see them hopping away from you as you walk through a meadow, consider carrying imitations in your box.

Behavior and Tactics

In the early morning, hoppers are less active than they are midday. Fish Para-Hopper, Dave's Hopper, or Joe's Hopper dry-fly patterns close to stream banks, where a real hopper could inadvertently jump or fly into the water. Cast the flies with enough force to create a small, rippling disturbance when they hit the water. It's effective to fish hoppers as the lead fly in tandem with small- to medium-sized nymphs, using the grasshopper as a strike indicator.

Notes

Immature grasshoppers of larger species as well as small species of grasshoppers are also available to trout. Small (#12–14) grasshopper patterns (also imitated by large caddis patterns or small Stimulators) can work very well. Many stonefly patterns do double duty as grasshopper patterns, and the fish may take hoppers for stoneflies, or stoneflies for hoppers. Some grasshoppers can fly great distances. Hoppers keep their wings folded over their back at rest.

Premier Hatches

All streams in Pennsylvania's farmland regions

Crickets

Cricket

Order: Orthoptera; Family: Gryllidae
#8–12, 2XL (12–25 mm)

Dave's Cricket

Hook: #8–12, 2X-long dry fly
Thread: Black 6/0 Uni-Thread
Tail: Black yarn loop under black deer hair fibers
Body: Black yarn
Palmered Hackle: Black, trimmed short
Wing: Black turkey wing quills
Legs: Trimmed and knotted black hackle
Head and Collar: Spun black deer hair, trimmed square at the head with excess fibers left for the collar

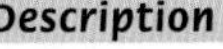

Description

Crickets have long, thick bodies, powerful rear legs, and two prominent antennae. Field crickets are larger than the smaller crickets common in the woods. Crickets are usually black or dark brown.

Emergence

Crickets are available to trout from late spring through the summer, until the first or second hard frost. They are found throughout Pennsylvania, but are particularly plentiful along streams adjacent to forests. Start carrying crickets when you hear their distinct chirp in the evening.

Behavior and Tactics

Crickets are more active in low light than grasshoppers. For anglers, crickets are the woodland version of the grasshopper (though crickets and grasshoppers can often be found occupying the same habitat). Fish them like you do hoppers, casting them at likely spots, with a pronounced "splat." A Dave's Cricket or Letort Cricket imitation works very well for prospecting with a dry fly.

Notes

Many anglers report better success with cricket imitations than grasshoppers on Pennsylvania streams. The Letort Cricket, designed by Ed Shenk, is another superb cricket pattern that can also be adapted to imitate grasshoppers.

Premier Hatches

Most trout streams, but they are particularly prevalent along streams that flow through wooded areas.

Beetles

Japanese beetle

Order: Coleoptera
#12–20 (3–20 mm)

Hi-Vis Crowe Beetle

Hook: #12–20 standard dry fly
Thread: Black 8/0 Uni-Thread
Body: Peacock herl
Wing: Black deer hair
Head and Legs: Trimmed black deer hair
Indicator: Pink foam

Description

Beetles generally have rounded or elongated oval bodies and two pairs of wings that they keep tightly folded on top of their backs when at rest. Many of the most common angler-significant beetles near trout streams are black with hints of green on their underside. But the Japanese beetle, which can be prolific along some trout waters, has a metallic green head and legs. Its underside is black, and its wings are metallic copper.

Emergence

Beetles are available to trout from late spring, through the summer, until the first or second hard frost. They are plentiful throughout all regions of Pennsylvania. Japanese beetles are active when spotted Joe Pye weed and bull thistle are blooming and when the gypsy moth caterpillars change into adults.

Behavior and Tactics

Cast a Hi-Vis Crowe Beetle imitation close to a stream bank or in-stream structure, such as a downed tree, with enough force to create a gentle "plop" when it lands on the water's surface. Expect trout to strike the fly as soon as it hits the water. During the summer and early fall, fish a larger beetle pattern (#10–12) as an indicator fly with a small nymph dropped off the bend.

Notes

Beetles are the largest order of insects in the world and the most prolific life form on the planet. In addition to black beetles of all sizes, lightning bugs, Japanese beetles, and ladybugs can all be important trout foods. Many beetles are aquatic and live much of their lives in the water.

Premier Hatches

Most Pennsylvania trout streams

Moths and Caterpillars

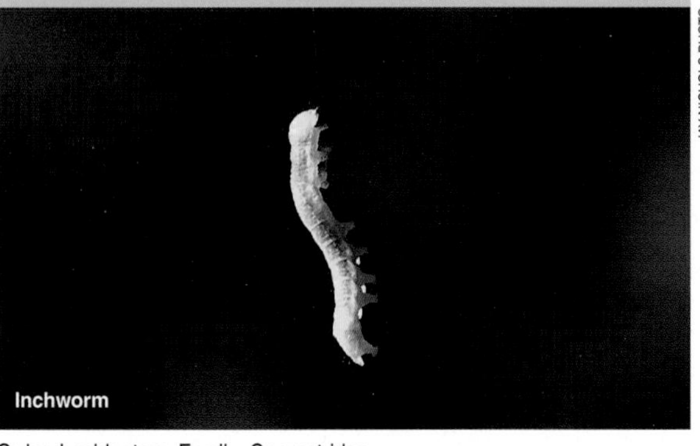
JAY NICHOLS PHOTO

Inchworm

Order: Lepidoptera; Family: Geometridae
#8–16, 2XL (10–40 mm)

Muddled Head Caddis

Hook: #6–12, 2X-long dry fly
Thread: Tan 8/0 Uni-Thread
Body: Tan beaver dubbing
Wing: Deer or elk hair

Green Weenie (inchworm)

Hook: #10–16, 2X-long nymph
Bead: Gold or copper
Thread: Chartreuse 8/0 Uni-Thread
Tail: Looped chartreuse chenille
Body: Chartreuse chenille

Description

Caterpillars are thick-bodied, wormlike creatures that are usually covered in fine, stiff hairs. They can be many different colors, depending on their species and diet. Inchworms have smooth, hairless bodies that are often colored green, brown, or black. Moths (adults) are often gray, brown, or a powdery tan color, but they can have a wide range of color, depending upon species. They have broad wings and thick, substantial bodies that are often the same color. Anglers sometimes mistake moths for caddisflies.

Emergence

Caterpillars and moths, including inchworms, gypsy moths, and forest tent moths, are common throughout Pennsylvania's forest regions. Their transformation from caterpillar to moth is usually a summer event. Inchworms dangle from tree limbs in mid-May and June. The adult moths are most active early on summer mornings and at night. Gypsy moth caterpillars are active when wild geranium is blooming and adult moth when the wild sarsaparilla blooms.

Behavior and Tactics

Inchworms can be prolific along trout streams where they dangle precariously from tree limbs by their silk lines. Many inchworms fall into the water, providing trout the opportunity to eat them. Green Weenies and other sunken inchworm patterns fished under an indicator dry fly work very well starting in late spring through summer.

Large caddis fly patterns work well for most caterpillar and moth adults. Fish them with a dead drift or an occasional subtle twitch. The naturals aren't always important in every region, even those where moth and caterpillar infestations are heavy.

Premier Hatches

Most Pennsylvania trout streams in forested areas

Damselflies and dragonflies are common on many trout streams and lakes in the state.

JAY NICHOLS PHOTO

9 Other Important Insects

Though their hatches are minor, you may encounter two additional insect groups along the trout stream: dobsonflies, fishflies, and alderflies in the order Megaloptera, and damselflies and dragonflies in the order Odonata. It's important to be able to identify them because trout eat their larvae when they are available.

Dobsonflies and Fishflies

Adult dobsonfly

JAY NICHOLS PHOTO

Dobsonflies (the adult form of the hellgrammite) and fishflies (Corydalidae family) are large insects, from 25 to 90 mm in their larval stage. They generally live in well-oxygenated riffles in the lower reaches of trout streams, where the water tends to be warmer. Alderflies (Sialidae family) are smaller, from 10 to 25 mm as larvae. And they are most commonly found in slow-moving water. All of these flies have complete life cycles (including a pupal stage), but most of their cycles are completed outside of the water. Because of this trait, pupa and adults are generally unavailable to trout. But their larvae live underwater from one to three years, and trout will eat them. The effectiveness of black Wooly Buggers may be due to the pattern's close resemblance to Megaloptera larvae.

Adult fishfly

JAY NICHOLS PHOTO

Damselflies and Dragonflies

JAY NICHOLS PHOTO

Damselflies and dragonflies (Odonata order) have incomplete life cycles, and their nymphs, which range from 10 to 60 mm, begin hatching in late spring. They are commonly found in lakes and ponds, but they also live in slow-moving sections of some Pennsylvania trout streams and rivers. The Upper Delaware River has a particularly large population of damselflies and dragonflies. It's common to see their adults dive-bombing the river in late May and early June, eating Sulphurs and Green Drake duns. The adults are generally unimportant to Pennsylvania fly anglers, because trout seldom eat them. Trout do eat the nymphs when they begin migrating toward dry, streamside vegetation, logs, or rocks to emerge.

PAUL WEAMER PHOTO

The nymphal stages of damsels and dragons (left) are important trout foods.

Appendix: Fly Pattern Recipes

Mayfly Spinners

Poly Wing Spinner

Hook: #8–14 2XL Daiichi 1230, or #14–18 1XL Montana Fly Company 1230
Thread: 8/0 Uni-Thread
Tail: Microfibetts
Body: Beaver dubbing
Wing: Gray polypropylene yarn
Note: Use thread and dubbing colors to match natural's body; synthetic or natural tailing fiber colors to match the natural's tails

Weamer's Truform Spinner

Hook: #8–14 2XL Daiichi 1230, or #14–18 1XL Montana Fly Company 1230
Thread: 8/0 Uni-Thread
Tail: Microfibetts
Body: Beaver dubbing
Wing: White or gray Antron
Hackle Post: Antron
Hackle: White or grizzly
Note: Use thread, dubbing, and hackle post colors to match natural's body; synthetic or natural tailing fiber colors to match the natural's tails; and grizzly hackle if the natural has prominent wing venations.

Stroup's CDC Wing Spinner

Hook: #8–24 Daiichi 1170 or 1180 (1280 for 2XL bodies)
Thread: 8/0 Uni-Thread
Tail: Medium dun hackle fibers
Abdomen: Antron dubbing
Wing: Medium dun CDC
Thorax: Peacock herl
Note: Use thread and dubbing colors to match natural's abdomen.

Hackle Wing Spinner

Hook: #8–24 standard or 2X-long dry fly
Thread: 8/0 Uni-Thread
Tail: Medium dun hackle fibers
Abdomen: Beaver dubbing
Wing: Badger hackle
Thorax: Peacock herl
Note: Use thread and dubbing colors to match natural's abdomen.

Sunken Spinner

Hook: #6–22, 2X-heavy scud
Thread: 8/0 Uni-Thread
Bead: Copper
Tail: Microfibetts or light dun hackle fibers
Abdomen: Turkey biots or dubbing
Wing: Clear Medallion Sheeting or light dun Antron
Thorax: Dubbing
Note: Use thread, abdomen materials, and thorax dubbing to match natural.

Simple Mayfly Nymphs

Beadhead Pheasant Tail

Hook: #6–22 nymph or 2X-heavy scud (for curved nymphs)
Bead: Gold
Thread: Dark brown 8/0 Uni-Thread
Tail: Pheasant tail fibers
Abdomen: Pheasant tail fibers
Rib (optional): Fine, oval copper wire
Thorax: Peacock herl
Wing Case: Mottled turkey wing quill
Legs (optional): Pheasant tail fibers

Flashback Pheasant Tail

Hook: #6–22 nymph or 2X-heavy scud (for curved nymphs)
Thread: Dark brown 8/0 Uni-Thread
Tail: Pheasant tail fibers
Abdomen: Pheasant tail fibers
Back: Pearl Flashabou accent
Rib: Copper ultra wire
Thorax: Peacock herl
Wing Case: Pearl Flashabou
Legs: Pheasant tail fibers

Hare's Ear

Hook: #6–22 nymph or 2X-heavy scud (for curved nymphs)
Thread: Black 8/0 Uni-Thread
Tail: Brown woodchuck or partridge
Body: Natural Hare's Ear dubbing
Rib: Flat gold tinsel
Wing Case: Mottled turkey wing quill

Beadhead Hare's Ear (Olive)

Hook: #6–22 standard nymph or 2X-heavy scud (for curved nymphs)
Bead (optional): Gold
Thread: Olive 8/0 Uni-Thread
Tail: Brown woodchuck or partridge
Body: Hare's Ear dubbing, dyed olive
Rib: Flat gold tinsel
Wing Case: Mottled turkey wing quill

Caddis and Other Nymphs

Anderson's Bird of Prey Caddis

Hook: #12–20, 2X-heavy scud
Bead: Gold
Thread: 8/0 Uni-Thread
Tail: Natural Hungarian partridge
Rib: Pearl Flashabou accent
Body: Rabbit dubbing
Hackle: Natural Hungarian Partridge
Thorax: Peacock herl
Note: Use thread and dubbing to match the natural's body color, which is usually green, olive, or tan.

Standard Beadhead (Caddis Larva)

Hook: #10–22, 2X-heavy scud
Thread: 8/0 Uni-Thread
Thorax: Rabbit dubbing
Rib: Fine, oval gold or copper wire
Head: Rabbit dubbing
Note: Use thread and thorax dubbing to match the natural's body, which is usually green, olive, or tan; use dubbing for the head to match the natural, which is usually dark gray, black, or brown.

Walt's Worm

Hook: #12–22 standard nymph or 2X-heavy scud (for curved nymphs)
Thread: Tan 8/0 Uni-Thread
Body: Natural hare's ear dubbing mixed with clear or light dun Antron

Copper John

Hook: #6–18 standard nymph
Bead: Gold
Thread: Rust 8/0 Uni-Thread
Tail: Black goose biots
Abdomen: Copper wire
Thorax: Peacock herl
Wing Case: Wapsi Thin Skin and a strip of Flashabou—coated with epoxy
Legs: Partridge or henback

Prince Nymph

Hook: #6–18, 2X-long nymph or 2X-heavy scud (for curved nymphs)
Bead (optional): Gold
Thread: Black 8/0 Uni-Thread
Tail: Brown goose biots
Rib: Oval gold tinsel
Body: Peacock herl
Wing: White goose biots
Hackle: Brown

Scuds and Sowbugs

Beadhead Olive Scud

Hook: #12–18, 2X-heavy scud
Bead: Gold
Thread: Olive 8/0 Uni-Thread
Tail: Olive hackle fibers
Wing: Olive Scud Back
Over Wing: Pearl Krystal Flash or Flashabou
Body: Olive Hare's Ear dubbing
Rib: Green Ultra Wire

Day's Burnt Back Sowbug (tied by Josh Day)

Hook: #12–20 scud
Thread: Black 8/0 Uni-Thread
Body: Light Wapsi Sowbug dubbing (melted on top with a heated needle to form a shell)
Legs: Trimmed olive hackle
Rib: Fine oval copper wire

Small Stoneflies

Kyle's Yellow Sally Nymph

Hook: #10–14, 2X-heavy scud
Thread: Tan 8/0 Uni-Thread
Bead: Gold
Tail: Brown goose biots
Abdomen: Tan beaver dubbing
Back: Orange Antron
Rib: Copper wire
Thorax: Chartreuse beaver dubbing
Wing Case: Black Thin Skin
Legs: Natural partridge
Antenna: Brown goose biots

Copper John (Rubber Leg)

Hook: #10–18 nymph
Bead: Black, copper, or gold
Weight: Lead wire
Thread: Black 8/0 or 70-denier
Tail: Rubber legs or black goose biots
Abdomen: Black Ultra Wire (Brassie)
Wing Case: Black Thin Skin and silver Flashabou coated with epoxy
Thorax: Bronze or black dubbing
Legs: Round black rubber legs (extra small)

Large Stoneflies

Jumbo John (Black)

Hook: #6–10 Tiemco 2499 SP-BL
Bead: Salmon-pink brass bead
Weight: .020-inch-diameter lead wire
Thread: Black 8/0 or 70-denier
Tail: Black goose biots
Abdomen: Black Ultra Wire (medium)
Wing Case: Black Thin Skin and pearl saltwater Flashabou covered with epoxy
Thorax: Peacock or black dubbing
Legs: Black round rubber legs (medium)
Collar: Black hen saddle

Rubber Leg Beadhead Stonefly Nymph

Hook: #4–14 Daiichi 1730
Bead: Gold
Thread: Tan or black 8/0 Uni-Thread
Tails/Antennae: Brown or black goose biots
Body/Thorax: Yellowish-brown or black rabbit dubbing
Rib: Gold or black V Rib
Wing Cases: Mottled turkey wing quill, coated with Softex and trimmed to shape
Legs: White, yellow, or black round rubber
Note: The Daiichi 1730 is a bent-shank stonefly hook.

Index

Note: Page numbers in **boldface** refer to detailed descriptions.